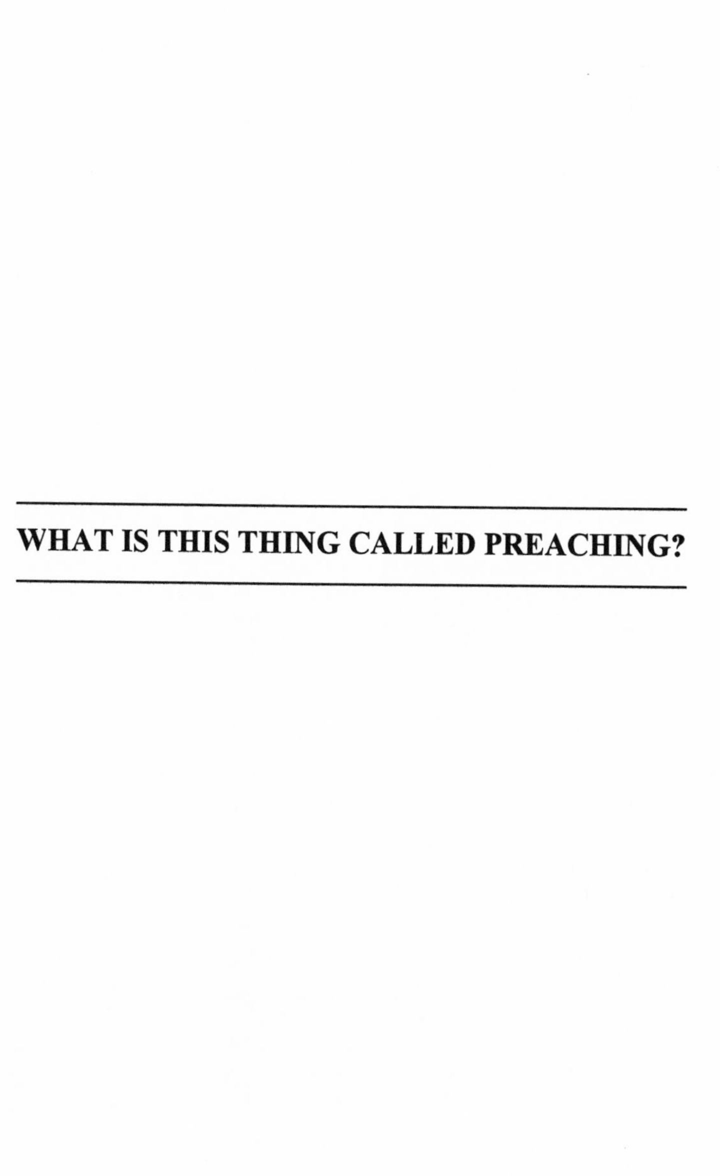

WHAT IS THIS THING CALLED PREACHING?

WHAT IS THIS THING CALLED PREACHING?

An Authentic Collection of Sermons

by Rev. Leon Johnson

Volume One

Leon Johnson

Rev. Leon Johnson

Leonidas A. Johnson

Rev. Dr. Leonidas A. Johnson

CRYSTAL FOUNTAIN PUBLICATIONS

DIAMOND BAR, CALIFORNIA

WHAT IS THIS THING CALLED PREACHING?
An Authentic Collection of Sermons by Rev. Leon Johnson
Volume One

Cover Design: Gail Oliver

Library of Congress Catalog Number: 96-85843

ISBN: 1-889561-01-0

Printed in the United States of America

TABLE OF CONTENTS

CONTENTS

But
even if
our gospel is veiled,
it is veiled to those who are perishing,
whose minds the god of this age has blinded,
who do not believe, lest the light of the gospel of the

glory of Christ,

who is the image of God, should shine on them.
For we do not preach ourselves,
but Christ Jesus the Lord,
and ourselves your
servants for
Jesus'
sake.

For
it is the God
who commanded light
to shine out of darkness
who has shone in our hearts
to give the light of the knowledge of

the glory of God in the face of Jesus Christ.

But we have this treasure in earthen vessels,
that the excellence of the power
may be of God
and not of
us.

[2 Cor. 4:3-7]

Special thanks to

Elaine Oliver-Graves

This Book of Sermons is Published to

The Glory of God

and to the memory of my hero

and idol in the ministry,

my father,

Rev. Herbert Leonidas Johnson

and his wife, my mother,

Rachel Bryant Johnson

and also to my faithful, and loving wife

Dolores Antonia Johnson.

Rev. Leon Johnson

This book is dedicated to my earthly father,

Rev. Leon Johnson

who, along with my mother, Dolores A. Johnson taught me

about

my heavenly Father,

my royal heritage in Jesus

and His indwelling Spirit in my Life.

In deep appreciation for his commitment to the ministry,

our family and for his example of how to be a humble,

holy, faithful, obedient, follower of Jesus Christ.

To Worthington and Esther and their families.

To Crystal D. and Alexander L. Johnson.

To God be the Glory!

Amen.

Rev. Dr. Leonidas A. Johnson

PROLEGOMENON

Warning:

> *...the word of God is living and powerful, and sharper than any two-edged sword, piercing even to the division of soul and spirit, and of joints and marrow, and is a discerner of the thoughts and intents of the heart.* [Heb. 4:12]

Historical Perspective

A brief look at the past may help you construct a historical foundation upon which you may perform the mental gymnastics of critiquing this book as a literary project. Looking back involves viewing the sum total of the genetic, environmental, and supernatural (spiritual) factors that have not only shaped me into who I am but also revealed to me whose I am. These factors include my familial, ethnic, and spiritual heritage.

Historical Perspective: Familial Blessings

The sermons in this book were originally composed by my father, Rev. Leon Johnson (1928-). My grandfather was also a preacher. His name was Rev. Herbert Leonidas Johnson (1896-1966) and he founded and pastored the Gloryland Baptist Church of New Orleans, Louisiana. My father tells me that my great grandfather, John Johnson (ca1866-?), served as chairman of the Board of Education in Sunshine, Louisiana. His position in the church is uncertain. Johnson family history beyond my great grandfather in North America is lost to factors related to the practice of slavery in this country. Even though my great grandfather escaped slavery, born around the time of the Emancipation Proclamation, the suffering, suppression, and oppression of African-Americans in the United States of America, especially in the deep South, is a significant part of my familial heritage.

The Johnson family has a strong tradition of active service in the Body of Christ. Various roles include pastor, associate minister, evangelist, minister of music, deacon, deaconess, mother's board, gospel artist, prayer warrior, and faithful church member. While some have not been as active as others, I believe the Johnson family, as a whole, demonstrates the generational blessing that can result from the power of prayer.

Active service in the Body of Christ is not restricted or limited to the Johnsons. For example, there is the Rev. Joseph Cager, my maternal great grandfather. He was a very tall giant in the ministry. How proud and fortunate we are to have had so great a personality to be a part of our lives. To God be the glory!

The conclusion of this matter is simply this, as a family, we may be hard pressed on every side, but we will not be crushed; we may be perplexed, but we will not drown in despair; we may be persecuted, but we will not be forsaken; we may be struck down, but we will not be destroyed! Why? Because where there is much prayer, there is much power, where there is little prayer, there is little power, and where there is no prayer, there is no power. The family that prays together, stays together.

Historical Perspective: History of Oppression

My ethnic heritage and familial heritage is colored with the dark experience of oppression. Many of my African ancestors, like many of my relatives, also suffered psychological trauma, emotional shock, and mental anguish as a result of institutionalized slavery. African men, women, boys, and girls where brutally hunted, captured, and forcefully torn from family, friends, and the familiar surroundings of their homes. They were beaten, emotionally abused, shipped to strange places, and exploited as slaves throughout the world.

Whereas information of my more recent ancestral heritage is hidden in the dark dreary shadows of institutionalized slavery and all the related experiences associated with living in bondage, the Bible records that my more ancient ancestral heritage shines with splendor and all the related experiences commensurate with dominion and power. Many Biblical scholars recognize Noah's son Ham as an ancestral father of the Black race. The descendants of Ham were politically, culturally, and technologically advanced and dominated the known world the first two thousand years of world history.

Historical Perspective: History of Deliverance

God has delivered many of my fellow African-American brothers and sisters who suffered unmerciful tragedies (physically, mentally, emotionally, and socially) both in this country and in other countries around this world. God has delivered millions out of the dark and delivered them into His marvelous light. He not only can deliver you from physical bondage but also mental, emotional, and spiritual bondage. By grace through faith you too can be saved. But, if the liberating news of the Gospel be hid, it is hidden from those who remain in bondage, have been blinded by the god of this age, and are perishing. The main point is this, ***God is a strong deliverer*!** He has proven what He can do time and time again. Since God has surrounded each of us with such a great a cloud of witnesses, let us be encouraged. What He has done for others, He can surely do for you.

Historical Perspective: Spiritual Heritage

I was born in the United States of America in 1959 and was raised in a Christian home by loving, supportive parents. I am a U.S. citizen. I was born again in the Kingdom of God, after 1959, and ever since, I have been guided through life by my Heavenly Father. My new citizenship is in Heaven. Spiritual birth is God's doing and it is a marvelous thing! My spiritual heritage is rooted in Jesus Christ. Because He lives, my hope is built on nothing less than Jesus' blood and His righteousness. Ever since my spiritual birth into the family of God, old things have passed away; behold, all things have become new. I am now a sojourner and pilgrim in a foreign land. I realize that this is not my home. One of these days, and it won't be long, you'll look for me and I'll be gone. I'm going up yonder, to sing and shout, nobody there is going to put me out! Come and go with me, to my Father's house. Everybody is welcome, but you must be, you got to be, born again.

Historical Perspective: The Call

When I started this project I was an ordained deacon. By the time I completed this project, I was a licensed minister. As I worked on this project, God worked on me!

This project represents one phase in God's carefully thought out and meticulously calculated plan to gradually bring to my awareness, through spiritual growth and maturity, His call for me to preach the Gospel of Jesus Christ.

Significant opportunities for spiritual growth and maturity were afforded me at Friendship Baptist Church (Yorba Linda, California), Talbot School of Theology at Biola University (La Mirada, California), and Watts Health Foundation, Inc. (Los Angeles, California). I am indebted to all the people affiliated with these institutions.

When the time had come, God put in my heart a desire to check out some of my father's sermons. Unknown to me, at the same time, God spoke to my father through others who encouraged him to publish some of his sermons.

God's plan came together in wonderful fashion. Once I started working on this project, my Heavenly Father spoke to my heart at various times and in different ways about preaching the Gospel. At first, these thoughts were only occasional, but then, the thoughts increased in both frequency and intensity. They became more intense as a result of the various issues going on in my life (issues concerning church life, work life, school life, family life, personal life, and finances).

I was unsure and unclear as to exactly what God was telling me to do. I questioned God as to whether it was necessary for me to announce that He had called me to the ministry. I was already involved in ministry as an ordained deacon and I had already enrolled in seminary school and had been taking classes for a number of years as a part-time student.

One day, as I labored through the intellectual contractions surrounding the issue of whether God was calling me to the ministry, a verse came to mind that gave birth to peace about the whole issue. It was the voice of Jesus saying:

> *In My Father's house are many mansions; if it were not so, I would have told you. I go to prepare a place for you. And if I go and prepare a place for you, I will come again and receive you to Myself; that where I am, there you may be also.* ***And where I go you know, and the way you know.***
> [John 14:2-4]

It was as though He was saying,

> Leonidas, you know where I live and you know that where I live is your home. You know that Heaven is your home and there is no danger that you will get lost as you travel home. **You know the way!** Therefore, I want you to know that I am giving you the responsibility of leading others home with you and I want you to be recognized as one I have chosen. Don't worry about who is and who is not following you. Don't worry about what other people say or do. **You know the way!**

Preaching and the Task

The task of writing this book brought to surface several unique tensions. One tension relates to the fact that the preaching event is a multisensory phenomena. To convert a dramatic and dynamic sermon to a static literary form was a major concern.

A second tension relates to the aim/purpose of preaching. If the aim/purpose of preaching is both to relay a message from God *and* to effect learning, then the preacher must also be viewed as a teacher, the listener as a learner, the physical church sancutary/auditorium as a learning environment, and the preaching event as a learning experience.

A third tension relates to the idea that the preached sermon is a unique, living phenomena that can never be duplicated. Each time a sermon is preached, it is shaped by external and internal factors acting upon the preacher-teacher, listener-learner, and the physical environment at a specific point in the time-space-matter continuum. Therefore, putting a preached sermon in a literary form that matches the original intent and essence of the original preached sermon required prayerful consideration.

I have made every attempt to preserve the originality and authenticity of the sermons. However, from time to time it was necessary for me to make some (not all) grammatical corrections and augment the sermons with scriptural references and refined theological and doctrinal teachings. At other times I merely amplified what was already present in note form. In other words, when needed and as led by the Spirit, I reinforced the columns of the sermon structure and added flesh to the sermon's skeleton.

Preaching and the Physical Realm

As humans, we have been designed with the ability to collect information about the physical world in which we live. We use our five sense to collect this valuable information. As you may recall, the five senses are vision, hearing, touch, smell, and taste. We can use these senses to learn about truth. What is truth? God's word is truth (John 17:17).

The preached word should not merely be an oral-aural event. In a learning situation, the more senses we employ, the greater the potential for discovery and the more effective learning will be. This is due to the many different learning styles different people possess. Expanding the potential for sensory stimulation during a sermon should increase the overall potential effect on the mind, emotions, and will of the listener-learner.

Because preaching is primarily an oral-aural event, people who are more effective at processing information aurally would exhibit the most potential to learn.

A form of communication that serves as a source of additional sensory stimulation is the non-verbal communication from the preacher. I am not referring to moments of silence or what the preacher chooses not to say in relation to what the preacher does say. These two situations are aurally discernible. This requires only the sense of hearing. I am referring to what the preacher physically does and does not do. These situations are visually discernible with the eye, requiring the sense of vision. The movements, the gestures, the play-acting of the preacher, etc., represent a very important component of the sermon. The congregation is constantly processing meaningful visual information through their sense of vision. The use of the sense of vision greatly enhances the effect of the sermon by adding vision with the sense of hearing. This facilitates learning for people who process information better visually. Visual learners as well as auditory learners will have an heightened potential to learn.

When the preacher asks the saints to praise the Lord, they may do so within their hearts. However, if the preacher asks them to give the Lord a praise clap and to say: "Praise God!" and they do it, the preacher has successfully added the sense of touch, along with the sense of hearing and the sense of vision, to the delivery of the sermon. Likewise, if the preacher tells the members of the congregation to turn their problems over to Jesus and leads them to do so symbolically by having them to write their problems on a sheet of paper, and then having them to physically lump that sheet of paper into a ball, and then having them to physically throw or discard that ball of paper at the alter, the preacher has introduced the sense of touch in the sermon. Another example of introducing the sense of touch is when the preacher tells the members of the congregation to stump on the floor as though they are stumping on the power of Satan in their lives (by virtue of their new identity in Christ). Again the preacher has employed the sense of touch. This would facilitate learning for those who process information better with physical activity and involvement. The addition of the sense of touch through physical movement and activity would benefit the kinesthetic learner. Having involved more senses in the delivery of the sermon, the preacher has increased the potential for discovery and effective learning by the listener-learner.

Likewise, the sense of smell can also be stimulated in the preaching event. For example, the smell of candles burning during service with the sweet smelling aroma of frankincense may be appropriately and strategically used when the topic of the sermon involves the gifts presented to the child Jesus by Magi. The sense of smell can also be stimulated in the listener by the preacher psychogenically by psychologically recalling in the mind of the listener an aroma that causes a real physiological effect. Even though there is no aroma present physically, in the mind, there is, and there is a real physiological reaction. The negative power of psychogenic phenomena is evident in illness, the positive power of psychogenics is evident in the miraculous and wondrous works of God.

The same would be true of the sense of taste. Eating, chewing, and/or sucking on something during a sermon to involve the sense of taste is not being advocated.

However, psychogenically, the preacher may directly focus in the mind of the listener something that physically stimulates their taste buds. For example, thinking about Sunday dinner (that roast in the oven, macaroni & cheese, collard greens, yams or going out to Sunday brunch) can literally cause a physiological response. If this is done, properly and appropriately, then the preacher has involved the sense of taste in the preaching event. As an example, this may be applied when preaching about the temptation of Jesus to turn stone to bread.

Reducing the sermon from a multisensory event to primarily single sensory processing event downgrades the use of our senses from a possible five to one (vision). Furthermore, when we read a sermon, we are visually impaired. We are partially sighted in that we lose physical nonverbal communication of the preacher and others in the environment (e.g., expressions, gestures, play-acting, reactions to the preacher from others...). We also lose the sense of sound (aural), and some potential for touch/feel, smell, and taste. Even though there is some possibility psychogenetically to employ other senses while reading a sermon, for the most part, when we read a sermon, in terms of our senses, we become visually impaired, deaf, and numb. If fact, we've lost the action, color and exaggeration of the preaching event.

Preaching and the Human Soul

Not only is the sermon a phenomenon that involves the physical aspects of human nature but it also encompasses the non-physical aspects of human nature which consist of: (1) The soul (mind, emotions, and will); and, (2) The spirit (God consciousness). The symbiotic like relationship between the physical and the non-physical nature of humanity also precludes the conveying of the full essence of a sermon into a literary form. We have to acknowledge the physiology that constitutes the basis for non-physical attributes in humanity. In doing so we must admit that the affect of the sermon on the non-physical aspect of human nature (soul and spirit) is inseparably related to the sermon's affect on the physical aspect of human nature through the five senses.

Preaching and the Drama of Worship

The *call-and-response-to-celebration* aspect of worship, typical of traditional African-American preaching, must also be considered when attempting to convert a sermon into a literary form. By *call-and-response-to-celebration*, I am referring to the congregational participation in the sermon event by various climactic responses such as:

1. Help'em Lord!
2. Well?
3. That's all right!
4. Yes s'ah!
5. Yeah y'ah Right!
6. Amen!
7. Glory!
8. Hallelujah!!

These responses may also involve physical gestures, such as waving hands, waving handkerchiefs, throwing handkerchiefs toward the preacher, tugging on the preacher's robe, standing, or even approaching the altar. Not only does the preacher give verbal and non-verbal communication that the congregation must receive aurally and visually, but the preacher is also a recipient of aural and visual sensory stimulation from the congregation's verbal and non-verbal communication.

The traditional African-American preacher *calls* for a *response* from the congregation. The preacher and the congregation depend on each other in this dramatic and dynamic form of preaching. Biblically based worship of God is dramatic. In true worship there is a dynamic dialogue between God and man. In true worship the One and Only, True and Living, God of the universe *calls* for a *response* from man, the crown of His creation. God initiates the first step, man responds, God initiates the next step, man responds, and the dynamic, rhythmic process of *call-and-response* between God and man continues, increasing in momentum and intensity to the climax where man leaves this call-and-response encounter rejoicing, shouting, and celebrating.

The interplay between the verbal and non-verbal communication on the part of the preacher and the verbal and non-verbal communication on the part of the congregation is an important component of preaching that helps the preacher-teacher and listener-learner journey up Calvary's Hill to an authentic encounter with Light of Life. This Holy Hookup (i.e., spiritual encounter) affects the body, soul (mind, emotions, and will), and spirit (God consciousness) of the Believer.

Considering the *call-and-reponse-to-celebration* nature of worship, one can begin to realize the restrictions and limitations one encounters when trying to portray a living, dramatic, and dynamic sermon in a seemingly lifeless, by comparison, literary form. If it were not for the Spirit of God, I would think this task to be futile. Isaiah (Isaiah 6:1-8) and John (Rev. 1:10-11) offer testimony that this project is not a futile venture for, *"God is Spirit and those who worship Him must worship Him in spirit and truth"* (John 4:24).

Preaching and the Sound of Music

Oral communication and written communication is quite different. Written communication has the luxury and goal of being succinct, short, and employs the economical use of words. Congruence of thought is seen by paragraphs and other visual clues. Oral communication is the opposite. Oral communication requires a different strategy to separate main ideas. Paragraphs must be heard, not seen. Important ideas and points must be repeated in different forms so that they are heard. Words and phrases must be repeated. The sound of the delivery is critical. If it doesn't sound right to the ear, one can not just re-read the sentence or paragraph as in written communications, therefore, the poetic, rhythmic, and melodic nature of verbal communication becomes important.

Even if one were to accurately record the meter and musical flow of words used to emphasize and bring to life the Spiritual truths preached, it would be difficult to convey into literary form the many sounds that surround the preaching event.

Preaching and Specialized Spiritual Factors

The spontaneous and dynamic movement of the Holy Spirit on the preacher-teacher, listener-learner, and the preaching-learning environment would inhibit the capture and confinement of the preached sermon to literary form. Instead of calling the literary sermons in this book "sermons" a more accurate term might be *sermon notes*. However, this term might be too misleading.

The actual preached sermon is a living, dynamic, phenomenon that takes form at the time of delivery by the Spirit of God. The various needs of the congregation and the preacher at the time of delivery are factors which God considers when He declares not only the purpose but the end results of a particular sermon.

Preaching: A Living Phenomenon

Difficulties in conveying a sermon into a literary form basically springs from the fact that the preached sermon is a living, melodic, holistic phenomenon that is extremely powerful, multi-faceted, and multi-dimensional in its makeup. Its essence can not be captured in lifeless, tone-dead ink.

The preaching event is a living phenomenon because the word of God is living and powerful. The preaching event is alive and full of action and color because God is alive, active, and creative. The preaching event is alive because the Spirit of God dwells in the believer.

Preaching and Carnival Thoughts

The preaching event may be likened to the celebration of a *Jolly Good Fellow*. When truth has revealed evidence of pure, loving, and heroic qualities in an individual, it is not uncommon to celebrate these high virtues in an almost carnival style fashion. People will gather from miles around to join in and witness the celebration. At some point the crowd ends up singing in unison,

> For he's a jolly good fellow,
> for he's a jolly good fellow,
> for he's a jolly good fel-low,
> which nobody can deny!

In the preaching event, who's the *Jolly Good Fellow*? Jesus! Jesus is the *Jolly Good Fellow*. God the

Father, Son, and Spirit is the ultimate "Jolly Good Fellow! However, the focus of this celebration is on Jesus, The Lamb of God who takes away the sin of the world! The preached sermon represents a carnival-like celebration of the one who's name is called, Wonderful, Counselor, Mighty God, Everlasting Father, Prince of Peace, the one which nobody can deny.

I can write about a "Jolly Good Fellow" party and try to describe it to you but the statement, "You had to be there," says it all. The statement, "You had to be there," can rightly be applied to the preaching event. In attempting to describe a particular sermon, we must often comment, "You ought'a been there." Even if you are chastised by God through the sermon, the good news remains, God is good, all the time! God is *The Jolly Good Fellow*, in the face of Jesus, "That Nobody Can Deny!"

The implication that a sermon can be conveyed into a literary form misrepresents the true nature of the sermon as an all encompassing worship experience.

Concluding Thoughts

Despite these special difficulties, I am confident that the conversion of the sermon notes into literary form will served to glorify God. The ultimate factor that will determine the success of this project and any sermon, regardless of shape, form, or fashion, is the Spirit of the Most High God. The Holy Spirit is supremely responsible for accomplishing the purposes of God in preaching. No matter what barriers, no matter what difficulties, no matter what methods used, no matter what techniques, no matter what style of preaching, no matter what form, no matter what skill or lack thereof, God's Spirit is ultimately responsible for accomplishing the results God has purposed.

God says,

"For My thoughts are not your thoughts, Nor are your ways My ways," says the Lord. "For as the heavens are higher than the earth, So are My ways higher than your ways, And My thoughts. For as the rain comes down, and the snow from heaven, And do not return there, But water the earth, And make it bring forth and bud, That it may give seed to the sower And bread to the eater, So shall My word be that goes forth from My mouth; It shall not return to Me void, But it shall accomplish what I please, And it shall prosper in the thing for which I sent it." [Is. 55:11]

I must testify that in the process of thinking through the difficulties involved in conveying a sermon into a literary form, God has let the Light from the Lighthouse shine on me. For this I am truly grateful and to Him I offer my praise to His glory.

God works in mysterious ways, His Glory to Behold!

Reverend Dr. Leonidas A. Johnson (1959-)

FOREWORD

I am grateful to Almighty God, our Heavenly Father, for giving me the inspiration, ability, inclination, and desire to make a positive contribution to the Christian ministry and to the cause of our Lord and Savior Jesus the Christ, by the means of these written and published sermons.

I make no claim to be unique or original. The ideas and contents for these sermons, although primarily and fundamentally biblically based in nature, came from both the religious community and the larger secular society as well, and at different times and circumstances during any twenty-four-seven-day-week period.

Some of these sermons were written with a great deal of relative ease. That is to say, prompted by the Holy Spirit, my thoughts, as related to sermon preparation, were coming out of my mind so fast and profusely, I could hardly write them. At other times, it was like shooting blanks. This is to say, that when I thought I was ready and prepared to write, nothing happened. I would sit, think, and pray for long periods of time. It seemed as though my mind had become tabularasa. At any rate, at such times, my efforts would yield no more than a paragraph or two, if that much. However, and at no time and under no circumstances was an attempt made to write a sermon without fervent prayer and the guidance of the Holy Spirit.

My concern and prayer is not to display, or show off, artistic skill, proficiency in writing, or the lack of it, but to establish a direct connection or correlation to the personal lives of those who preach the word, those Christians who hear the Gospel, and also to the non-Christians in society at large. In other words, the word must be relevant to our day and time. It is my prayerful concern that these messages be relevant to the ethos of the day, and remain true to the scriptures upon which they are based.

It would be foolish, dishonest, and disrespectful if I attempted to claim credit for this work. Let's face it, we all need help. We all depend upon one another and vary in degree of need. In this case, and in the first place, it was God's Holy Spirit who provided the inspiration, thoughts, and ideas. To God be the glory, for the things He has done.

Secondly, to my ever loving and faithful wife, Dolores, for a steady, ever-flowing source of constant encouragement. Also to numerous, sincere fellow well-wishing Christian believers who heard some of these sermons and encouraged me to publish them in a book.

Many thanks to Reverend Dr. Leonidas A. Johnson, my son, for his long hours of labor, dedicated to the editing and formulation of this book.

Reverend Leon Johnson (1928 -)

Chapter 1

WHAT IS THIS THING CALLED PREACHING?

Scripture: 1 Cor. 1:17-29; 1 Cor. 2:1-9; 1 Cor. 15: 1-5;
2 Tim. 4:1-8

Songs: 1. *Great is Thy Faithfulness* (Thomas O. Chisholm)
2. *At the Cross* (Issac Watts - Ralph Hudson)
3. *A Charge to Keep I Have* (Charles Wesley)

Have you ever seriously wondered what it is about preaching that would cause you and others to drag your tired body up out of bed, get dressed, and rush to a certain church on a particular Sunday morning? Haven't you ever heard someone say, "Rev. 'So-n-So' is going to be preaching today over at 'such-n-such' a place. You know it's going to be crowded. Don't be late if you want to get a good seat." Who is Rev. 'So-n-So' ? What does he have to do with your getting out of bed? Do you go to church to hear Rev. 'So-n-So' sing, pray, moan, hoop, holler, and wax mightily, or, do you go to get a message from Lord God Almighty? If you go to church to get a message from the Lord, you go for the right reason. If you go to hear Rev. 'So-n-So' preach because you just wanted to hear him, then this message should be interesting. It is entitled, "**What is This Thing Called Preaching?**"

When a person is identified or referred to as a preacher, what images or impressions come to your mind?

Do you think of that person as a money-grabber? A womanizer? A self-seeking flimflam con man? Or, do you think of that person as a sincere, honest, polite, gentle, humble, type of person? Do we think of a preacher as being somewhat different, a peculiar person who has some special relationship with God? These are just some impressions people have of preachers. Today I want to focus your attention on one preacher all ministers should be compared to. That preacher is the Apostle Paul. But, before we go too far, let us be clear in our thinking about what a preacher is. A preacher is a **messenger**. He delivers messages from God.

Let's take a look at that famous preacher, the Apostle Paul. Some of the people at Corinth were suspicious of Paul's motivation for what he was doing. So the Apostle Paul made it very clear what he was about. Listen to what he wrote in his letter to the church at Corinth:

> *And I, brethren, when I came to you, did not come with excellence of speech or of wisdom declaring to you the testimony of God. For I determined not to know anything among you except Jesus Christ and Him crucified.*
> [1 Cor. 2:1-2]

Let's now take a look at some of us who call ourselves preachers. Some of us have, by the grace of God, gone to many of the finest colleges, universities, and seminaries in the land. We have picked up a few new words, and learned the meaning of the same. We have taken a few courses in philosophy, psychology, and theology along with other subject areas. The names and work of such men as Plato, Aristotle, and Socrates are not unfamiliar to us. We are not ignorant of the names and works of such great men as Karl Barth, Emil Brunner, and Reinold Niebuhr. We know of Paul Tillich and Rudolf Bultman. We are acquainted with the philosophical thinking of the Romantics, the Realist, and the Existentialist, just to name a few. Having had this experience, some of us feel as though we know more, or at least as much as the teachers and the professors who taught us.

We have ministers in the pulpit today with a vocabulary and eloquence that would make that great Roman orator Cicero green with envy. We call these silver tongue orators pulpiters. Today we have ministers who are more sophisticated than the mighty Apostle Paul, more learned than the Greek philosophers Socrates and Plato. But sophistication and eloquence is their total package. There is no Holy Ghost power and no conveyance of conviction. On an intellectual or emotional level, the natural or carnal man may say he preached a good sermon but the spiritual man will say something was missing. As a consequence of this, many preachers are more style than substance. Eloquent speech may or may not sound good and convincing but does it heal the sin-sick soul?

Keen intellect and impeccable speech has nothing to do with the saving grace of God. To be sure, someone has to speak the word but, it need not be perfect for God's grace to work its effect in our lives. For by grace are we saved through faith, it is the gift of God. And beside that, keen intellect and brilliant philosophical awareness is no guarantee of sound doctrine and the faithful preaching of the gospel. Behind some eloquent speech and soothing words we may find another Jim Jones or David Koresh.

Until we preachers come to the point where we can truthfully say like Paul, I am determined, not simply persuaded, not simply convinced, but determined to know nothing but Jesus and him crucified, we will continue to have 'great' or so called 'great' pulpiteers who can, hoop, holler, moan, sing, use big fancy words like, exegetical analysis, and wax mightily, but with no Holy Ghost power or conviction.

Paul wrote in Rom.10:14-15 that a preacher is a messenger sent to proclaim the ***gospel of peace*** and ***to bring glad tidings of good things!*** We proclaim and deliver messages from God inspired by His Spirit and our diligent study of the Scriptures of the Old and New Testament. We are to be wise as serpents and calm as doves.

Most importantly, we have to remind ourselves to be careful and not get caught up in the popular thought of the day. You know the one I am thinking about, the, "We don't do that anymore. This is a new day. We are a new and different generation. We have a new agenda." Be on the alert. This could be a trick of the devil. Indeed, for many peoples, this is nothing but a trick bag. Our Bible teaches us that God changes not. He is the same yesterday, today, and tomorrow. We cannot allow ourselves to be persuaded by whatever popular opinion is in vogue at the time. It is in this context that we must remind ourselves of Paul's charge:

> *Now this I say lest anyone should deceive you with persuasive words. For though I am absent in the flesh, yet I am with you in spirit, rejoicing to see your good order and the steadfastness of your faith in Christ. As you have therefore received Christ Jesus the Lord, so walk in Him, rooted and built up in Him and established in the faith, as you have been taught, abounding in it with thanksgiving. Beware lest anyone cheat you through philosophy and empty deceit, according to the tradition of men, according to the principles of the world, and not according to Christ. For in Him dwells all*

the fullness of the Godhead bodily; and you are complete in Him, who is the head of all principality and power. [Col. 2:4-10]

As the saying goes, "if it ain't broke, don't fix it!" In Paul's letter to the church at Colose, he specifically challenged and warned them to be on the lookout for, and not to be taken in by the philosophies and vain deceit of men.

To the church at Galatia Paul wrote,

Paul, an apostle (not from men nor through man, but through Jesus Christ and God the Father who raised Him from the dead), and all the brethren who are with me, To the churches of Galatia: Grace to you and peace from God the Father and our Lord Jesus Christ, who gave Himself for our sins, that He might deliver us from this present evil age, according to the will of our God and Father, to whom be glory forever and ever. Amen. I marvel that you are turning away so soon from Him who called you in the grace of Christ, to a different gospel, which is not another; but there are some who trouble you and want to pervert the gospel of Christ. But even if we, or an angel from heaven, preach any other gospel to you than what we have preached to you, let him be accursed. As we have said before, so now I say again, if anyone preaches any other gospel to you than what you have received, let him be accursed. For do I now persuade men, or God? Or do I seek to please men? For if I still pleased men, I would not be a servant of Christ. But I make known to you,

> *brethren, that the gospel which was preached by me is not according to man. For I neither received it from man, nor was I taught it, but it came through the revelation of Jesus Christ.* [Gal. 1:1-12]

One of our big problems in the church is vain preachers in the pulpit. We are not content to preach the simple, but full gospel. We somehow feel we have to embellish, add to, amplify, or, somehow modify the gospel, to make it more attractive, more palatable to its would be listeners. Do we think we are giving the Lord some needed help, or doing Him some special favor when we add this humbug foolishness to his precious word? The Lord did not call philosophers to preach -- he called preachers who can take directions and follow orders. If we are serious about this matter of preaching we do well to heed Paul's admonition. Philosophy may be interesting, and we may learn a thing or two, but a time will come when we must give an account for our stewardship. Paul wrote to the church at Corinth:

> *Let a man so consider us* [preachers], *as servants of Christ and stewards of the mysteries of God. Moreover it is required in stewards that one be found faithful.*
> [1 Cor. 4:1-2]

Today you don't hear many sermons preached on heaven or hell and fewer ones on sin. As one psychologist wondered, "What ever happened to sin?" Sermons of today seem to emphasize everything but the heart of the matter of the human condition, which is sin. God's judgment is seldom, if ever, mentioned. When is the last time you heard a real sermon on grace or repentance? We are preaching a superficial message that is soothing to the ear, the emotions, and intellect but reaches not the soul. We are preaching and perpetuating a perverted gospel.

We know that:

> *...the Word of God is living and powerful, and sharper than any two-edged sword, piercing even to the division of the soul and spirit, and is a discerner of the thoughts and intents of the heart.* [Heb. 4:12]

Also;

> *All Scripture is given by inspiration of God, and is profitable for doctrine, for reproof, for correction, for instruction in righteousness that the man of God may be equipped for every good work.*
> [2 Tim. 3:16-17]

We ministers, who call ourselves preachers, need not try adding to the Word of God's effectiveness by putting our little two cents change in. It is a two-edged sword affecting the preacher and the hearer. The same message delivered to the same audience has different effects. Some hearers are ecstatic with joy, others are mad as 'H' 'E' double 'L'. For some hearers the message is too long, for other hearers, sitting in the same congregation, hearing the same preacher deliver the same message, the sermon is too short! *"We are fools for Christ's sake,..."* (1 Cor. 4:10). but if we are faithful and obedient to God in our ministry, not only will the children of God become wise in Christ but they will also become strong in the Lord and the power of His might.

Then too, we must ever be conscious of who we are, whose we are, and what we are about. This is made very plain to us in the tenth chapter of Romans. Paul made the statement: *"For 'whoever calls upon the name of the Lord shall be saved'"* (Rom. 10:13). Then he asks:

> *How then shall they call on Him in whom they have not believed? And how shall they believe in Him of whom they have not heard? And how shall they hear without a preacher? And how shall they preach unless they are sent? As it is written: 'How beautiful are the feet of those who preach the gospel of peace, Who bring glad tidings of good things!* [Rom. 10:14-15]

God calls the preacher, equips the preacher, prepares the preacher, and sends the preacher out to preach authentic messages from Heaven, which are drawn from the sacred Scriptures of the Old and New Testament. Nobody, and I mean nobody, is capable or qualified to add to or subtract from God's Word. In Paul's letter to the Galatians he writes, "*But even if we, or an angel from heaven, preach any other gospel to you than what we have preached to you, let him be accursed*" (Gal. 1:8). We are complete in knowing nothing but Jesus Christ and Him crucified.

It is from the faithful preaching of the Word of God, that we learn the meaning of life, who we are , whose we are, how we got here, where we are going, as individuals and as a group. We did not come into this world as consequence of some freak accident or chance. It was no freak of nature, in other words, it was not by evolution. You and I were created in the image and likeness of God. He, God, created us in His own image. The Holy Scriptures tell us that God loves you and me.

It is in God's Word where we can find our real value and our true worth. So what: you don't have a lot of money, you don't have nice clothes, you don't have a fancy, expensive car or you don't have one at all, you don't live in a big house; you don't have a terrific education, you don't have a glorified job or you don't have employment at all, you don't have a husband, you don't have children, you don't have a father, you don't have this, you don't have that. Too many people are caught up trying to keep up with everybody else. The local church is full of people trying to keep up with the "Jones'." You know them, they are the ones that will add up the things that you don't have and conclude consciously or subconsciously, you, or anybody like you, aren't worth much, if anything at all.

God looks at those 'things' you don't have and says, "So what, those things don't give you value!" What do 'things' have to do with how much you are worth to God? Your home is in Heaven. As a child of God, your true value according to God is evident by the historical fact that your heavenly Father, loved you enough to send His only begotten Son, Jesus, to die in your place for the remission of your sins. Jesus was crucified, hung, suffered, bled, and died on Calvary's cross that you and I might be redeemed and given the opportunity to go home one day to celebrate and enjoy being in the presence of our Lord and King, Jesus Christ.

You may not hear this good news from the people you hang out with and if you don't read or study the Bible, how would you know that God has a plan for your future, a plan of hope? God want's you to know about His wonderful plan of salvation designed especially for you and He has given this message to the preacher. If the preacher is faithful and obedient to God, he will deliver this message to you truthfully. Now, if you abide in His word, you can verify the consistency of the message with Holy Scripture as you are led by the Spirit of God who dwells in every child of God. If you abide in His word, Jesus said, *"...you shall know the truth and the truth shall make you free"* (John 8:32). It is from the preaching of the cross we learn more about God, who He is, what He has done for us and what He promised to do for us, where He is, why we are here, and when we can stop worrying about our problems.

It pleased God that by the preaching of the cross the shackles of doubt and cynicism are destroyed.

> My faith looks up to Thee,
> Thou Lamb of Calvary
> Savior divine!
> Now hear me while I pray,
> Take all my guilt away,
> O let me from this day Be wholly Thine!
> *My Faith Looks Up to Thee* (Ray Palmer)

It pleased God that by the preaching of the cross faith, hope, and love are established and maintained. When you become a child of God, all things become possible with the approval of your heavenly Father. Remember God's message the Apostle Paul delivered in Phillipians 4:13, *"I can do all things through Christ who strengthens me."* Nothing is too hard for God!

By the preaching of the cross we learn something of the extent of God's love for us. John 3:16 reads,

> *For God so loved the world that He gave His only begotten Son, that whoever believes in Him should not perish but have everlasting life.*

1 John 3:1 reads,

Behold what manner of love the Father has bestowed on us, that we should be called children of God!

God's love for us is so high, you can't get over it, so low, you can't get under it, and so wide, you can't get around it. In Romans 8:35-39 Paul delivered this message:

> *Who shall separate us from the love of Christ? Shall tribulation, or distress, or persecution, or famine, or nakedness, or peril, or sword? As it is written: 'For Your sake we are killed all day long; We are accounted as sheep for the slaughter.' Yet in all these things we are more than conquerors through Him who loved us. For I am persuaded that neither death nor life, nor angels nor principalities nor powers, nor things present nor things to come, nor height nor depth, nor any other created thing, shall be able to separate us from the love of God which is in Christ Jesus our Lord.* [Rom. 8:35-39]

It pleased God that by the preaching of the cross, sinners come to repentance and the redemption of their soul. If you are lost in sin, the preached word proclaims that Jesus will take you in and shine the light from Heaven in your soul. Just have a little talk with Jesus, He's the only one that can make your life whole.
The bible teaches that,

> *For since, ...,the world through wisdom did not know God, it pleased God through the*

> *foolishness of the message preached to save those who believe.* [1 Cor.1:21]

And to that man, woman, boy, or girl who dares to ***believe*** the message of God preached by the preacher ***and*** who ***accepts*** Jesus as their personal Lord and Savior through faith, God says, "*...he is a new creation; old things have passed away; behold all things have become new*" (2 Cor. 5:17).

By the preaching of the cross burnt out lives are revitalized and energized.

> We praise Thee, O God,
> for the Son of Thy love,
> For Jesus who died and is now gone above.
> Hallelujah, Thine the glory!
> Hallelujah, amen!
> Hallelujah, Thine the glory!
> Revive us again.
> *Revive Us Again* (William P. Mackay)

It is by the preaching of the cross that we are able to sing, "I Ain't No Ways Tired." It was from the faithful preaching of God's word that the shackling walls of slavery came tumbling down. That kind of existence cannot be maintained when God's word is preached faithfully with power and conviction.

It is by the preaching of the cross that the liberating news of God's gospel is made known. We were once sinners - held captive by the power of sin. But Jesus says,

> *Come to Me, all you who labor and are heavy laden, and I will give you rest. Take My yoke upon you and learn from Me, for I am gentle and lowly in heart, and you will*

find rest for your souls. For My yoke is easy and My burden is light. [Matt. 11:28-30]

When we hear the gospel preached things begin to be seen in a new light. Our mind set changes from earthly things to heavenly things, from the flesh to the spiritual, from darkness to His marvelous light. Old things are passed away and all things become new.

These are just a few reasons why Paul said, *"...woe is me if I do not preach the gospel!"* (1 Cor. 9:16) and why preachers must take the charge to preach seriously. We must preach the word in season and out. We must not stop or let up. We must preach when we are happy. We must preach when we are sad. We must preach when we have a crowd. We must preach when we have a faithful few. We must preach when they listen, we must preach when they don't. We must preach like our iife depended on it. We must preach because somebody's life does depend on it. We must preach like its our last time.

This may be the last time,
this may, be the last time,
this may, be the last time,
it may be the last time I don't know.
Traditional

Preaching days won't last forever. We must, *"...work the works of Him who sent* [us] *Me while it is day; the night is coming when no one can work"* (Matt. 9:4).

One of these days, and it won't be long,
you'll look for me, and I'll be gone.
I'm going to Glory, to sing and shout,
nobody there is going to put me out!
Traditional

By and by when the morning comes,
When the saints of God are gathered home,
We'll tell the story how we've over come;
For we'll understand it better by and by.
We'll Understand It Better By and By
(C.A. Tindley)

I want to be like Paul. I want to be able to say, *"I have fought the good fight, I have finished the race, I have kept the faith"* (2 Tim. 4:7). I want the crown of righteousness that is laid up for me, which the Lord, the righteous Judge, will give to me on that Day, and not to me only but also to all who have loved His appearing. Most of all I want to hear the Master say, "Well done thy good and faithful servant. Well done!"

Chapter 2

THE QUALITY GOES IN BEFORE THE NAME GOES ON

Scripture: Jeremiah 1:4-10; 2:4-13

Songs: 1. *If I Can Help Somebody* (A. Bazel Androzzo)
2. *I Am on the Battlefield for My Lord*
(Sylvana Bell & E. V. Banks)

Jeremiah was a prophet that lived during the latter part of the seventh century B.C., and the first part of the sixth century. During his long ministry, more than forty years, he warned the nation of Israel, and more specifically, the Southern Kingdom called Judah, of the catastrophe that was to fall upon them because of their idolatry, wickedness, and sin.

For background information, you may recall that Abraham begat Isaac, and Isaac begat Jacob, who's name was changed to Israel, and Jacob's children formed the twelve tribes of Israel, which became the Hebrew nation, or the nation of Israel. They were united as one kingdom under King Saul, King David, and King Solomon. The nation of Israel split, however, after King Solomon's reign into the Northern Kingdom, called Israel and the Southern Kingdom called Judah. The Northern Kingdom immediately turned away from the worship of Jehovah to idolatry and adopted as their national religion Calf-Worship, the religion of Egypt. Soon afterward they added Baal-Worship, which was a fertility or sex cult. The

Northern Kingdom was soon carried away in captivity by the Assyrians because of their idolatry and wickedness as God had warned through His prophets. The Southern Kingdom, which included the Holy city of Jerusalem and the temple, maintained faithful worship of Jehovah, the God of Abraham, Isaac, and Jacob. However, with time, Baal-Worship, idolatry, and iniquity spread to the Southern Kingdom.

Jeremiah warned the people and king of the Southern Kingdom that they would be destroyed by Babylon if they did not turn from their wicked, idolatrous, and sinful ways. In the third chapter of Jeremiah the northern Kingdom is likened to an espoused wife who has forsaken her husband for promiscuous association with men, making herself a common prostitute. In that same chapter, verse 14, God pleads to the Southern Kingdom through His prophet Jeremiah, *"'Return, O backsliding children,'...'for I am married to you...'"* (Jer. 3:14).

You may recall that at Mt. Sinai, after Jehovah, the God of the Hebrews, delivered them out of the land of Egypt with great wonders designed to show God's power and to declare in all the earth that He is The One and Only True and Living God, the Israelites promised to render total loyalty and obedience to Jehovah their God in return for His everlasting care and protection. This was a conditional covenant, or promise between God and the Israelites.

Let's take a look at Jeremiah's mission. Jeremiah was called by God to do a very specific job. God instructed Jeremiah to tell God's people that they have committed two evils: (1) they have forsaken God, The Fountain of Living Water; and (2) they have hewn themselves cisterns - broken cisterns - that can hold no water. In other words, like the Northern Kingdom who rejected the worship of Jehovah, the God of Abraham, Isaac, and Jacob, for idol worship, like the espoused wife who has forsaken her husband for promiscuous association with other men, making of herself a common prostitute, the Southern Kingdom had forsaken The One and Only True and Living God, The Fountain of Living Water, for idol worship.

Let's talk to Jeremiah regarding his mission. Jeremiah, your task seems simple enough. Jeremiah, tell the truth, tell it like it is, tell it like God said, don't hold nothing back. You know, the bible does say that Jesus came that we might know the truth and that the truth shall make us free (John 8:32). Jeremiah, even though the bible also says we should speak the truth in love (Eph. 4:15), love must be tough at times. Why? because, as the bible also says,

> *And this is the condemnation, that the light* [the truth] *has come into the world, and men loved darkness rather than light* [the truth], *because their deeds were evil.* [John 3:19]

Even with God, at times, enough is enough, and God, out of love, has to let his people know that they are slipping, they are becoming too complacent, and they are moving in the wrong direction.

Jeremiah, God must let them know that they are not growing, they are loosing their first love, and they are loosing sight of the goal. God must let them know that they are reneging on their promise or covenant with God and if they don't correct the situation soon, trouble will come. Jeremiah, God must let them know that night will soon fall. Jeremiah, God must let them know that a storm is approaching and that it will rain in their lives. Jeremiah, God must warn them that judgment is on its way.

Jeremiah, even though they might not want to hear the truth, it is for their own good. The truth exposes darkness of sin, and at times, most times, we, like Adam and Eve, are more interested in hiding our sins instead of confessing them in God's sight and light and forsaking them. Consequently, like roaches, we remain bound in darkness afraid of entering into His marvelous light and experiencing freedom.

Jeremiah, sometimes, you may get some favorable compliments. People may tell you they admire your sincerity, your straight forwardness, your courage, and boldness. But, Jeremiah, you should also know that telling it like it is, is not quite the same as hearing it like it is. Not too long after you get started, somebody is going to tell that you should mind your own business.

Jeremiah, someone is going to call you out of your right name. They will call you a pest, a pain in the neck, an agitator, a donkey's behind, and some other choice names. They will smile in your face and talk about you like a dog behind your back, especially your so-called friends.

Jeremiah, many will challenge you, some face-to-face, and they will ask, "What right do you have to say the things you are saying? When did you get the authority and who gave it to you? Who made you Judge? " Jeremiah, somebody is going to charge you with meddling in their affairs. The truth will expose all that which is hidden. Jeremiah, when that occurs, you will find yourself in the middle of a bunch of mess. You will be surrounded by heated anger and controversy. When you get to that point, Jeremiah, you know you are getting close to doing what God has assigned you to do. At that point, you must realize that is only the beginning.

Jeremiah, even some of God's elect will speak against you and get on your case. They will try to belittle you, and discredit your efforts. But don't be discouraged. Just keep right on pressing on. By that time you will begin to understand why God has chosen, prepared, and sent someone special - a specialist for the situation. Jeremiah, before spiritual surgery can be done, an incision has to be made. Socio-psychological defense and escape mechanisms must be anesthetized. The sin has to be exposed and removed before recovery and healing take place.

Jeremiah, God only uses carefully selected, highly trained specialist(s) for this type of work. God will only use someone who is qualified, someone He knows can and will get the job done. Before God sends someone to do a job for Him, you better believe that that person was carefully chosen and prepared for the task. Jeremiah, you have been chosen. *The Quality Goes In Before the Name Goes On* (Slogan for Zenith Electronics Corp.).

Jeremiah was a prophet. We find the test for a prophet in Deut. 18:20-22. There it states that every prediction of a true prophet must come true. False prophets were to be killed (Deut. 13:1-10).

Even though Jeremiah happened to be a priest and a prophet, the difference was that priests were a hereditary class but prophets were not. Priest became priest because their fathers were priest. They were not individually chosen but born into the job. There was no conviction of the heart required, just evidence that you were a direct descendant of Aaron, the High Priest. They were not elected and they could not be fired; therefore, their job security was tight, and the job benefits were great. God's people brought the best of the best, the cream of the crop, to the priest to present to God as offerings. God permitted the priest to live off a portion of these offerings (Num. 18:8-20). No matter if they did a good job, poor job, or no job at all, the people didn't have much recourse. It was basically up to God to handle poor leadership. Sounds like the attitude adopted by many New Testament church people today. That being, church people do not have much recourse for poor spiritual leadership, church leaders are accountable to God only and it's up to God, Himself, to deal with church leadership problems. Well, let's move on. Consequently, priests were often the most wicked men in the nation. Yet they were the religious teachers. But instead of preaching and teaching against the sins of the people, they joined in with them and became leaders in iniquity and wickedness.

Prophets were not so. Each individual prophet got his or her call directly from God. Their job was to speak, "What thus said the Lord God Almighty." Jeremiah, you have been chosen. *The Quality Goes In Before the Name Goes On.*

Jeremiah, the message that God wants you to proclaim is timeless. It has as much relevance today as it had when first uttered. Good not only for your generation, Jeremiah, but for ours as well. Too many people are doing the same thing. I must caution you, my brothers and sisters in Christ, my fellow coworkers in the gospel cause, preachers, deacons, choir members, ushers, Christian educators, and all who profess to be Christians, just because you go out in the name of the Lord, don't think because God is Love and you are in the church dealing with church folks, that it's going to be 'lovee-dovee', that every Christian you deal with will be nice, that you will be received with open arms, smiles, hugs, and kisses, that you will receive any appreciation for your labor of love, your sincerity, your truthfulness, your straightforwardness, or your boldness. If you expect all these things, then it's time for a reality check.

Jeremiah, when things get real rough, there may even come a time when you will be tempted to take Job's wife's advice to, "...Curse God, and die" (Job 2:9)! Just because Job's wife gave up, it does not mean you should. Did God choose Job's wife to do the task or did God call Job? If God called you to do a task, you are the one qualified to do it. It would be poor judgment to take the advise from someone who tells you to quit God's work.

When it's quitting time, God will let you know, until then, do not stop or quit the work of ministry.

Now, you should be careful to note, Jeremiah, that while God has special designs for your life, you should not think that you are the only one so privileged. God has many others who can claim a personal, intimate, relationship with Him, and many of them are faithful and work diligently in what they think to be His will. But, God has too many who have become enameled with their surroundings, blending in the mix, acclimating to popular socio-political thoughts and trends. They are just going along with the flow, which ever way the winds blows, to the point that they have forgotten who they are, whose they are and what they are supposed to be doing and why. That is where you, Jeremiah, come in. However, you are not to take over, as if everything has gone completely out of control. Things are in bad shape - there is no question about it. But God has already revealed His guidelines and laws and has given numerous illustrations and examples for God's people to follow. But, somehow, too many of God's people have found a way to ignore them, or pretend they, or even God, doesn't exist. Something has to be done, and God wants you to do it. Jeremiah, *"The Quality Goes In Before the Name Goes On!"*

It is not that the Israelites are against God. It is that way for some, but for others, it is more a matter of misdirection, misunderstanding, and mistakes in judgment. It's also a matter of apathy, complacency, lack of commitment, lack of courage, and lack of knowledge. Jeremiah, remember what God's wise servant King Solomon wrote, *"There is a way which seems right to a man, But its end is the way of death"* (Prov. 14:12).

Jeremiah, there is one more thing you must be careful about. In speaking to God's people with the authority God has vested in you, you face the real danger of becoming arrogant and presumptuous. Remember, you are addressing God's people, and, although they often go astray, this does not mean that God wants to destroy them. So speak the truth in love. Speak with confidence and authority, be as wise as a serpent and as calm as a dove.

Then, too, Jeremiah, remember the heart is deceitful and desperately wicked. God searches the heart, God knows it. God is authorizing you to declare that the God of Abraham, Isaac, and Jacob is the Living Water, and that they who drink of that water, shall never thirst. Water - pure, clean, refreshing - that runs to the very depth of the soul.

Tell them all, Jeremiah, that God hung the stars in the sky, created the sun and moon and caused them to shine down from the heavens above. God created man, breathed in him the breath of life, and man became a living soul.

Jeremiah, I know it is human for you to expect some positive fruit as a result of your labor. The work is long, hard, tiring, and anxiety producing but, don't be discouraged if you don't see immediate results because of your efforts. Remember God's faithful servant Noah and how long and hard he worked and what he had to endure from his peers. God's word will come to past. So, don't be weary in well doing. You shall reap, if you faint not. Your labor is not in vain!

Jeremiah, be strong in the Lord and the power of His might. Be assured, you are a part of the unbeatable combination: God and one faithful, obedient servant. In this combination you will experience life's experiences, ups and downs, sunny days and black midnights, joys and sorrows, aches and pain, battles large and small, victories and defeats, and plenty of mistakes so that when God gives you a specific task or assignment, you will be able to get the job done. For God will have chosen, prepared, and sent you, a specialist for that situation and God will continue to develop you to the fullest of your potential in all dimensions. In the end you will be able to declare, *"I have fought the good fight, I have finished the race, I have kept the faith"* (2 Tim. 4:7). Jeremiah, *"The Quality Goes In Before the Name Goes On!"*

Let's take a look at the conditions under which you must minister, Jeremiah. Its been nearly 75 years since Isaiah the prophet ministered to the Southern Kingdom of Judah. Because of Isaiah's work, Jerusalem was spared destruction. Isaiah lived in the reigns of King Uzziah through King Hezekiah. King Hezekiah was perhaps the best king in Judah's history. King Hezekiah brought religious reform to the Southern Kingdom. Even though Isaiah was able to spare the destruction of Jerusalem and the temple, the mighty Assyrians posed a constant threat. King Hezekiah was followed by king Manasseh, who ruled for 55 years. King Manasseh was wicked and perhaps the worst king in the history of the Southern Kingdom of Judah.

Jeremiah, as you may well know, God uses the rod of man to chastise His people. There has been a succession of different nations keeping the Jewish nation in submission by God's design. There were the Egyptians, Syrians, and during Isaiah's time, the Assyrians, the Babylonians, also known as the Chaldeans, who are now a growing world power.

Jeremiah, let's take a look at the changes that have taken place in the Southern Kingdom of Judah that have angered God and given Him cause to put them on notice. Let's look at what happened to the faith of Abraham, Isaac, and Jacob. Furthermore, let's investigate the possibility of a breach of contract of the covenant made at Mt. Sinai between God and the Israelites.

One thing we can note that happened, Jeremiah, is that King Manasseh instituted some sinful wicked ways that took away some of the moderate religious reforms that took place under his father, King Hezikiah. He did evil in the sight of the Lord, according to the abominations of the nations whom the Lord has cast out before the Hebrew nation. (see II Kings 21:1-7): God is not pleased! Jeremiah, *"The Quality Goes In Before the Name Goes On!"*

1. King Manasseh rebuilt the high places, that is, places for pagan worship, which, Hezekiah his father had destroyed. This meant the God of Abraham, Isaac, and Jacob was replaced by the worship of idols. Broken cisterns. God is not pleased! Jeremiah, *"The Quality Goes In Before the Name Goes On!"*

2. King Manasseh raised up altars for Baal and Asherah, fertility (sex) gods, as Ahab king of the Northern Kingdom had done. This meant they had forsaken God, the Fountain of Living Water - and hewn themselves 'broken cisterns' that can hold no water. God is not pleased! Jeremiah, *"The Quality Goes In Before the Name Goes On!"*

3. King Manasseh worshipped, all the hosts of heaven, that is, the gods of the Assyrians, and served them. Broken Cisterns. God is not pleased! Jeremiah, *"The Quality Goes In Before the Name Goes On!"*

4. King Manasseh built altars in the house of the Lord, of which the Lord had said, *"...In Jerusalem I will put My name"* (2 Kin. 21:4). And he built altars for all the hosts of heaven in the two courts of the house of the Lord. Broken cisterns. God is not pleased! Jeremiah, *"The Quality Goes In Before the Name Goes On!"*

5. King Manasseh also made his son pass through fire, practiced soothsaying, used witchcraft, and consulted spiritists and mediums.

> *He even set a carved image of Asherah* [a fertility goddess] *that he had made in the*

> *house of which the Lord had said to David and to Solomon his son, "In this house and in Jerusalem, which I have chosen out of all the tribes of Israel, I will put My name forever;* [2 Kings 21:7]

Broken cisterns. God is not pleased! Jeremiah is not pleased!

> *The Quality Goes In Before the Name Goes On!*
> *The Quality Goes In Before the Name Goes On!*
> *The Quality Goes In Before the Name Goes On!*

Well, history tells us that all of these changes, and more, were eyewitness accounts of Jeremiah during the forty years for which he prophesied for God. In 588 B.C., God allowed Jerusalem to be invaded by the Babylonian King Nebuchadnezzar. The walls of Jerusalem were torn down, the city destroyed, its temple ramshacked and many of its citizens either killed or enslaved and exiled to Babylon. The bible records that all but a small remnant remained. Jeremiah was one of the survivors. Together they fled to Egypt (Jer. 43.7).

Today, just as God needed someone special in Jeremiah's time, God needs some special, dedicated, committed, men and women to do the same thing Jeremiah did. God needs today's Jeremiahs to warn the people of their idolatrous, wicked, sinful ways which have caused them to forsake God the Father, Son and Holy Ghost, the Fountain of Living Water, and turn to broken cisterns which have no water. By God's grace, through faith in Jesus Christ, you have been chosen. You have been chosen. If you have professed a saving faith in Jesus Christ, the Son of God, you have been chosen.

At the moment you accepted Jesus Christ as your personal savior, God equips you with at least one spiritual gift for the work of ministry (1 Cor. 12:4-11). The Holy Spirit equips every child of God with at least one spiritual gift. Even as a brand new convert, you have been equipped and prepared, to some degree, to start working for God. As you study God's word and grow in the faith, your abilities and responsibilities will increase. You have been chosen and prepared for Kingdom building.

In Matt. 28: 19-20 Jesus says,

> *Go therefore and make disciples of all nations, baptizing them in the name of the Father and of the Son and of the Holy Spirit, teaching them to observe all things that I have commanded you; and lo, I am with you always, even to the end of the age.*

Jesus in the great commission has sent us out to do a job. You have been chosen by God the Father, prepared by God the Holy Spirit, and sent by God the Son. We are called ambassadors for Christ (2 Cor. 5:20). Because God calls us His ambassadors, we can rest assured, *The Quality Went In Before the Name Went On!* God made us special. God chose us to do something special. God has given us a special name. We are today's Jeremiahs. We are specialists, chosen, prepared, and sent to do God's work.

Crime of every description and category is on the rise. The divorce rate, teenage pregnancies, and gang-banging drive-by shootings are on an upward spin. Alcoholism and drug abuse are on the rampage. Homosexuals are coming out of the woodwork exposing a sin-infested political agenda. AIDS is dropping men and women like flies. Despair and hopelessness is clouding the vision of thousands trapped in urban and lower socio-economic communities. Corruption and destruction of Christian ethics are destroying the moral fabric of society. Apathy, decadence, and selfish ambition is common in political, social and spiritual leadership. Cult and satanic worship is on the rise. Evangelical theology and biblical interpretation is under attack. Racism and ignorance is still lurking about. God is not pleased! God is not pleased! Today's Jeremiahs,

The Quality Goes In,
Before the Name Goes On!
The Quality Goes In,
Before the Name Goes On!
The Quality Goes In,
Before the Name Goes On!

The quality has *gone in* you, now its time for you to *go on* and do what God has chosen you to do! The work for the servant of God is truly great. There are many lost souls in this world. The harvest is indeed plenty, but the laborers are few. All Christians have been chosen to minister in and out of the church, which is the body of Christ. Within the church we are to equip each other for the work of ministry for edifying the body of Christ (Eph. 4:11-16). All members of the body of Christ form a royal priesthood and, as such, we are to minister outside the church. We are called to proclaim the praises of God, who called us out of darkness into His marvelous light (1 Pet. 2:9).

The ministry of God is not to be casually considered. It got rough with Jeremiah. He experienced moods of inadequacy, doubt, and despair. When God's prophecy did not immediately materialized he became the laughingstock of his peers. He was ridiculed, ostracized, thrown in a pit and left to die, (but saved by an Ethiopian). He was extremely frustrated and wanted to quit the ministry. In fact, he even cursed the day he was born, but kept on living. Nevertheless, Jeremiah was a man of great faith and prayer and serves as a great inspiration to us all. Even though he wanted to quit, he didn't, he stayed on the battle field until he died. Listen to what he prays during one of his lowest moments as recorded in Jer. 17:14,

> *Heal me, O Lord, and I shall be healed; Save me, and I shall be saved, For you are my praise.*

Jesus Christ, our Lord and Savior, despite all of His Good and wondrous deeds, was ridiculed, ignored, misused, abused, and even crucified. We are His servants and a servant is no greater than his master. That is why the quality must go in before the name goes on. Fire purifies gold but destroys wood. The Gospel ministry is not for the phony, imitators, those who delight in perpetrating a fraud. In the end they will be burned.

Finally, remember, you Jeremiahs of today, all you preachers, all you teachers, all you deacons, all you trustees, all you choir members, all you ushers, all you who claim to be Christians, and that includes all you pew-sitting-bench-warmers, you must follow these directions before you can sit at the Master's feet and be blessed. As you travel this pilgrim way journey, keep your feet on the straight and narrow path of righteousness. It will lead you to the Street of Glory. Keep straight until you come to a junction, turn right, and that will put you on Holy Avenue. Stay on Holy Avenue for a good while, it will lead down through the valley. After you go through the valley you will come to a blend in the road, then you will be on Hallelujah Boulevard. Stay on Hallelujah Blvd. and you will run smack into King's Highway. As you travel King's Highway, you will see signs from heaven, and you may begin to feel a little strange. Put on your sunglasses because it will get very bright. By then, you will know that you have entered Gloryland. But stay on King's Highway because it leads you to the Throne of Grace. As you approach the Throne of Grace, the angels will inform you that you are stepping on Holy ground. Then you will soon hear a familiar voice, the voice of Jesus. Jesus - the King of kings and Lord of lords. Jesus - the Rose of Sharon. Jesus - the Lily of the valley. Jesus - the crucified, dead, buried, but risen Savior. Jesus - the Bright and Morning Star. The angels will be singing, *"...Holy, holy, holy - Lord God Almighty, Who was and is and is to come"* (Rev. 4:8)! Singing,

> *Worthy is the Lamb who was slain*
> *To receive power and riches and wisdom,*
> *And strength and honor*
> *and glory and blessing!* [Rev. 5:12]

So stay on the job preacher, choir member, usher, deacon, my brothers and sisters. Keep working for the Master. Keep proclaiming the unending riches of the Gospel. The quality has gone in. You have been chosen, prepared, and sent to serve in the army of the Lord. You are defenders of the faith, so put on the whole armor of God, that you may be able to stand against the wiles of the devil (Eph. 6:11). You have been purchased by the blood of the Lamb. You are the potter's clay molded by the hands of God (Jer. 18:1-11). People today are straying away from God, the fountain of Living Water, even denying Him for cisterns, broken cisterns that can hold no water. God doesn't like that! How does it make you feel? Today's Jeremiahs, the quality has *gone in* before the name has *gone on* you! Yes! You have been chosen! I have been chosen, you have been chosen, we all have been chosen, prepared, and sent by God the Father, Son, and Holy Spirit to do His will. We are a part of an unbeatable team and we will reap if we faint not (Gal. 6:9).

The Quality Goes In Before the Name Goes On!

Chapter 3

HEY! LOOK WHAT I GOT!

Scripture: Matt. 25:14-30; Acts 3:1-9

Songs: 1. *Give of Your Best to the Master* (Howard B. Grose)
2. *Open My Eyes, That I May See* (Clara H. Scott)
3. *Higher Ground* (Johnson Oatman, Jr.)

Many people are much more well off than they project themselves to be. We often cry poor-mouth, or emphasize what we don't have or can't do. Paradoxically, this seems to become more and more evident the higher one climbs the socio-economic ladder. The more we get, the more we want. We have been so influenced by our society to the point we think of ourselves as being in or out, up or down, rich or poor, a success or failure, important or unimportant, by our material possessions. There is no question that the size and balance of our bank account, the size, location and contents of our home, the make, model and year of our car, if we have one, the type of clothes we wear, where we shop, etc., have a lot to do with the way in which we see ourselves and the way other people view us.

Me? Go with you? In your car? You got to be joking -- I would not be caught dead in that rotten old jalopy! I don't want to talk to him. He looks and smells like a bum, you got to be kidding. I don't want to sit by her. She dresses like my grandmother. Me? sit by her? - I don't think so! I can't go to church. I don't have anything to wear. I wore that dress last week. What will people think? I want to go to church, but I'll be embarrassed. No way, I'm not going. He's nice, honest, and cute, why don't you go out with him? What? Me, go out with him? I want to, but he doesn't have a 'J.O.B.', 'C.A.R.', or an 'A.P.T.' (apartment)! Get the picture?

This morning, we want to emphasize the positives. Notice what Peter said, *"Silver and gold I do not have, but what I do have I give to you"* (Acts 3:6). The emphasis is not on the negative (what I don't have) but, rather on the positive (what I do have). Peter did have a firm belief in the Lord Jesus Christ and what Jesus could and would do for those who believed and trusted in Him. Peter did not focus on what he did not have but rather on what he did have and what he could and was willing to do with what he had. The emphasis is on the positive. What I do have I give to you.

There are some situations in which people have allowed what they don't have to be the controlling factors which guide their lives. It does not have to be that way. The dominant and controlling forces and activities of our lives should not be controlled by what we don't have. We need to stop putting ourselves down with a constant theme of negativity - I don't have this, I don't have that, we can't do this, we can't do that, - no one can gain any degree of height if they weigh themselves down with a constant stream of negative thoughts. It becomes too easy to fall into the trick bag of always wanting someone or something or some institution to take care of you. When you are constantly looking for handouts, you start loosing self confidence, initiative, dignity, and self respect.

Moses, that great patriarch of the Old Testament, complained to God about what he did not have and what he could not do when God told him to go down in Egypt land and set the children of Israel free. God told Moses to use what he had and not to worry about what he didn't have.

Moses was obedient and confronted the great Egyptian Pharaoh and his mighty army with only a staff and a rod. He could have buried himself with continued complaints about what he did not have and what he could not do, but he decided to use what he had and to let God work with and through him. Moses learned to use what he had. Well, the Bible tells us what happened in that situation. The people of Israel were set free and Pharaoh's mighty army drowned in the Red Sea. The bible teaches that God and one is a majority. *"Silver and gold I do not have, but what I do have I give..."* (Acts 3:6). It does make a difference when God is with you and you give what you do have.

Little David, play on your harp, --Hal-le-lu-jah; little David, play on your harp, -- Hal-le-lu-jah; little David, play on your harp, --Hal-le-lu-jah. Little David could have complained that Goliath, the Philistine giant, was much too big, much too strong, much too powerful for him to even think about accepting the challenge. Why even Israel's best warriors were afraid of Goliath and fled from him. Having accepted Goliath's challenge you would think the best thing David could have done was to run and pray that Goliath didn't take him seriously. Goliath took him seriously. David did not run and he did not hide. He did not register his complaints. Instead, he used what he had. He went forth in the name of the Lord with his sling and five smooth stones. Well, the bible documents what happened (1 Sam. 17). God was with little David. David prevailed and when the Philistines saw that their champion was dead, they fled. I said it once and I'll say it again, God and one make a winning team! *"Silver and gold I do not have, but what I do have, I give..."* (Acts 3:6). In this case, one sling and five smooth stones.

You mean to tell me we have to feed all of these hungry people! Why there must be thousands! Where are we going to get the food? The only food discovered here are five loaves and two fish. What good is that going to do? We simply do not have enough food to feed everybody. There is no way we can meet the needs of all these hungry people. Here's another situation in which apparent, legitimate complaints could have been registered. Well, the Bible documents what happened. The multitude was seated to be served as Jesus commanded. Not only did the five thousand get fed, but there were twelve baskets full of fragments and of fish as leftovers (Matt. 14:15-21; Mark 6:36-44). *"Silver and gold I do not have, but what I do have, I give..."* (Acts 3:6). In this case, five loaves and two fish. Give God what you have and leave the rest to God. Stop complaining about what you don't have!

Hey! Look what I got! What do you have Rev. Johnson? I got a mind. I don't have silver and I don't have gold but what I do have is a good mind. I woke up this morning clothed in my right mind. I got a mind! Someone once said, 'A mind is a terrible thing to waste'. Everything you and I see, was first conceived in somebody's mind.

Every mansion, skyscraper, cathedral, every yacht, ocean liner, every submarine, jet, airplane, spaceship, every school, campus, university, every hospital, every jail, every theme park, every resort hotel, every building, every poem, every book, every sculpture, every painting, every piece of art, every symphony, melody, piece of music, every dance, every movie, and so on was first conceived in somebody's mind.

We use our minds to think, and you don't need silver or gold to use it. It doesn't cost one dime, it doesn't cost one penny, it doesn't cost anything!

I woke up this morning with my mind,
stayed on Jesus
I woke up this morning with my mind,
stayed on Jesus

HEY! LOOK WHAT I GOT!

I woke up this morning with my mind,
stayed on Jesus
Hallelu... hallelu... hallelu-jeh!
Traditional

I got a mind! It has been said, 'If my mind can conceive it, and my heart can believe it, I can achieve it'! I got a mind, you got a mind, all of God's children got minds.

Scientists tell us that we only use ten percent (10%) of our minds capacity. This means, for one reason or another, we are not using our minds to full capacity. We are lazy, sleepy heads, constantly complaining about why we can't do this, and why we can't do that.

Hear me clearly, all books have not been written, all buildings have not been designed, all melodies have not been composed, all inventions have not been invented, all speeches have not been given, all presentations have not been made, all solutions and peace treaties have not been made, all teachings have not been taught, all cures have not been discovered. Humanity is always in need of a good mind. I got a mind, you got a mind, all God's children got minds. Let's use them more often. I'm going to use my mind to the glory of God. I am also going to follow the exhalation Paul made to the church at Phiilppi. He wrote:

> *Finally, brethren, whatever things are true, whatever things are noble, whatever things are pure, whatever things are lovely, whatever things are of good report, if there is any virtue and if there is anything praiseworthy - meditate on these things.*
> [Phil. 4:8]

"Silver and gold I do not have, but what I do have, I give..." (Acts 3:6). In this case, my mind.

Hey! Look what I got! I have eyes. So you have eyes Rev. Johnson. So what! Doesn't everybody have eyes? If that is true, then what are these things called eyeglasses, contact lenses, and magnifiers? Dr. Leonidas Johnson, my son, tells me that approximately 75% of what we learn about our surroudnings is through our eyes. Vision is the most valued sense we possess. I was awakened this morning by the finger of God's love and behold I saw the light of another new day. I have eyes that see. Thanks be to God who gives us the victory through Jesus our Lord and Savior. When my eyes (that see) send images to my mind (that works) you can believe I have a pretty good idea of what's going on around me. Behold, my eyes indicate to my mind and heart thy soul be on thy guard, ten thousand foes arise.

I've seen the lightening flashing
And heard the thunder roll!
I've felt sin's breakers dashing,
Which tried to conquer my soul;
I've heard the voice of my Savior,
He bid me still fight on -
He promised never to leave me,
Never to leave me alone.
Never Alone
(Source unknown, 19th century)

"Silver and gold I do not have, but what I do have, I give..." (Acts 3:6). In this case, my vision.

Hey! Look what I got! What do you have Rev. Johnson? I have ears to hear. You may say so what, big deal, everybody has ears Rev. Johnson. If everybody has ears, what is this thing called a hearing aid. I have ears that hear, not only what people say, but also what they don't say. When my ears (that hear) along with my eyes (that see) send their messages to my mind (that works), you can believe I have a good idea of what's going on in any given situation. *"Silver and gold I do not have, but what I do have, I give..."* (Acts 3:6). God has given me ears that hear and I am going to use them to the glory of His name.

Hey! Look what I got! I have a mouth that works. Whether you think I talk too loud, too soft, too long, too short, I can speak words of truth wrapped up in love. I can speak words of encouragement, words of comfort, words of joy, words of peace and forgiveness. And if I don't have anything good to say, I can keep my mouth shut. I can give the testimony:

I was sinking deep in sin,
Far from the peaceful shore,
Very deeply stained within,
Sinking to rise no more;
But the master of the sea
Heard my despairing cry,
From the waters lifted me
Now safe am I.

Souls in danger, look above,
Jesus completely saves;
He will lift you by His love
Out of the angery waves.
He's the Master of the sea,
Billows His will obey;
He your Savior wants to be
Be saved today.
Love Lifted Me (James Rowe)

Most importantly, I can praise God, who is worthy of all praises. *"Silver and gold I do not have, but what I do have, I give..."* (Acts 3:6). In this case the power of the tongue.

Hey! Look what I got! What else do you have Rev. Johnson? I have confidence and faith in God. I can do all things through Christ who strengthens me. I must confess, like other people, I sometimes become a bit concerned with the way other people see and think of me. I wonder from time to time, what impact my conduct, my walk, my speech, my mannerisms have upon the effectiveness of my ministry. After all, impressions and images do have a bearing on the effectiveness of one's effort. I am not alone in this regard.

Even Jesus had a concern relating to this matter and his ministry. On one occasion, Jesus called his disciples together and began to question them regarding what the people were thinking, what impressions did they have of Him. Then He asked Peter point blank, I want to know what you think? Peter responded, *"...'You are the Christ, the Son of the Living God'"* (Matt.16:16).

I trust that you will agree with me in this area as to how important images and impressions are. I hope you will also agree with me that much of what we hear and see in so many areas are pizzazz, sensationalism, a front, a show with very little substance or meaning, lacking depth, sincerity, genuine faith, and conviction. Yes, I have faith in God:

My faith looks up to Thee,
Thou Lamb of Calvary,
Savior divine!
Now hear me while I pray,
Take, all my guilt away,
O let me from this day
Be wholly Thine!
My Faith Looks Up to Thee (Ray Palmer)

HEY! LOOK WHAT I GOT!

I have confidence and faith in God, who does all things well. My Lord is too wise to make a mistake, and too loving to be unkind. This is why:

My hope is built on nothing less
Than Jesus' blood and righteousness;
I dare not trust the sweetest frame,
But wholly lean on Jesus' name.

On Christ, the solid Rock, I stand - All other ground is sinking sand,
All other ground is sinking sand.
The Solid Rock (Edward Mote)

"Silver and gold I do not have, but what I do have, I give..." (Acts 3:6). In this case, confidence and faith in God.

Hey! Look what I got! I have access to the throne of grace. My heavenly Father has promised me, in His word, he would supply my every need (Matt. 6:25-34) and if I delight myself in the Lord, He would give me the desires of my heart (Ps. 37:4; Matt 7:7-11). I can go to God in prayer. I can tell him what I need and want. I have a heavenly father, full of mercy and lovingkindness, who hears and answers prayers. Call Him up!

Jesus is on the main line, tell him what you want.
Jesus is on the main line, tell Him what you want.
Jesus is on the main line, tell him what you want,
Call Him up and tell Him what you want.

Call Him up, Call Him up, Tell Him what you want.
Call Him up, Call Him up, Tell Him what you want.
Call Him up, Call Him up, Tell Him what you want,
Call Him up and tell Him what you want.
Traditional

My heavenly father watches over me! His eye is on the sparrow and I know He watches me. *"Silver and gold I do not have, but what I do have, I give..."* (Acts 3:6). In this case, the power of prayer. *"The effective, fervent prayer of a righteous man avails much"* (James 5:16).

Hey! Look what I got! I have a special name given to me by my heavenly Father. I got a new name. I've got a new name, over in Glory and it's mine! I may be called Leon Johnson, the name my mother and father gave me. I may be called Leon, the name which my wife calls me. I may be called 'eon, the one called me by my little granddaughter, she is still working on the pronunciation. I may be addressed as Mister, Brother, or Reverend Johnson, all are all right with me. But I tell you, I got a new name over in Glory and it will sound better and have far greater sound.

There are some names that I have been called during the course of my life that I dare not mention from this pulpit. That's all right with me, I don't like those names, but I can deal with that. A lot of people need Jesus. You need Jesus, I need Jesus, we all need Jesus. Then, there are those names that people call me to my face and those they call me behind my back. I'm talking about so called friends and church folk. Again, no problem, I can deal with that, no big deal. I just recall what Jesus said,

> *Blessed are you when they revile and persecute you, and say all kinds of evil against you falsely for My sake. Rejoice and be exceedingly glad, for great is your reward in heaven, for so they persecuted the prophets who were before you.*
> [Matt. 5:11-12]

HEY! LOOK WHAT I GOT!

Leon is really a French name, and it means like a Lion. It was given to me by my earthly mother and father. My new name will be given to me by my heavenly Father. The time will come when I hope to hear the voice of my heavenly Father say, " Well done thy good and faithful servant." I got a new name, over in glory, and it's mine, mine, mine. I got a name, you got a name, all God's children got a name, when we get to heaven, God's going to give us our name, and we're going to shout all over God's heaven! *"Silver and gold I do not have, but what I do have, I give..."* (Acts 3:6). In this case, the knowledge that I have a new name over in Glory. My hope is that my new name will mean good and faithful servant of the Most High God.

Let's pause here for a monent, take inventory, and see just what we do have. Let's start with the basics. *One*, you woke up this morning to the light of another new day. Take my word for it, it was not the alarm clock that woke you up. God woke you up. You have life. *Two,* you were clothed, as the saying goes, in your right mind. You were fully conscious of who you are and what your plans were for the day. You got a mind. *Three*, you have eyes that see, even if you have to wear glasses. Count it a blessing. *Four*, you have ears that hear, even if you have to do so with the aid of a device. *Five*, you have a mouth and tongue that enables you to speak and communicate with others. Wow! That's fantastic! *Six*, you have arms, hands, and fingers - perhaps all in good working condition. Think of what your life would be like if all of these were impaired or missing. *Seven*, you have hope. You may have arthritis, rheumatism, heart problems, cancer, aids, or some other ailment, but, you are still alive. Where there is life, there is hope. Nothing is too hard for God. Nothing is too hard for God. Nothing is too hard for God. Then too, do not ever forget God's promises. Delight thyself in the Lord and he will give you the desires of your heart (Ps. 37:4; cf. Ps. 84:11; John

10:10). *Eight,* you have faith in God who has promised never to leave you or to forsake you. His eye is on the sparrow and I know he watches me. My heavenly Father watches over me. *Nine,* you can go to God in prayer. You can tell Him what you need. You can tell Him what you want. On top of that, God says in His word, *"...No good thing will He withold from those who walk uprightly"* (Ps. 84:11).

Now, to me, if you or I have all this, and we do, it does not sound like someone who is poor or who is in need. The song we sometimes sing in church, *How Rich I Am* most definitely had you in mind. So let's stop this nonsense, garbage talk about, I don't have this, I don't have that, we can't do this, we can't do that. We should always keep before us the thought of the song, *All Things are Possible if We Believe.*

Well, what does all this mean? What is the point? For one, we ought to get off this negative trip, the theme which is: "I can't do this and I can't do that." You and I may not have a staff and rod, a sling with five smooth stones, or two fish and five loaves of bread, but, we do have a mind, we do have eyes, we do have ears, we do have a mouth, we do have some degree of faith and confidence in God, we do have access to the throne of grace. All these things can be used to the glory of God. We also have a new name over in glory, which gives us a sense of direction, purpose, and a sense of who we are and whose we are.

Also, remember that God and one is a majority. God, our heavenly Father is the creator and sustainer of this universe. Nothing is too hard for God. The 'little' that we have to offer is not 'little' with God. Silver and gold we may not have, but what we do have to give, in the hands of God, can achieve exceedingly and abundantly above all we could ever dream or expect.

Remember too, the confidence Paul had in himself because of his faith in God. You and I can act the same way because of our faith in God. God expects no less from us. Let's not disappoint Him. Also, we should ever be prayerful to God, that He would open our eyes, that we may see glimpses of the truth Thou has for us, open our ears, that we may hear voices of truth, Thou has for us, and open our mouths and let us boldly proclaim the truth in love everywhere we go. *"Silver and gold I do not have, but what I do have, I give..."* (Acts 3:6).

The scriptural text for this sermon indicates God has not been so stingy, or narrow-minded, so as to be partial. His love is manifested in abundance. His grace abounds to every individual. God has given us all talents and skills. Some of us have one spiritual gift, others have more than one. You may have one combination of spiritual gifts, someone else may have another combination or mixture of spiritual gifts. Each child of God has a unique talent or number of talents or mixture of talents given to us by the Holy Spirit (1 Cor. 12:4-11). God is expecting positive results from talents he has given you, God is looking for a return on His investment.

For some reason many of us are not using our skills, abilities, and our talents. Many of us may not have this or that, but we do have something and we are guilty of not using what we do have. We have buried our God given gifts, abilities, and talents in the graveyard of indifference. Others have laid to rest their dreams, ambitions, and aspirations in the cemetery of 'I don't have this-or-that'. Still, others have thrown their hope and confidence in God into the fiery furnace of king 'I can't do this-or-that'. All this in the face of, *"I can do all things through Christ who strengthens me"* (Phil. 4:13). Auhh...Ohh...! Hoo...Whee...! Somebody's going to get it! Somebody's in trouble! How much money did it cost you to receive your God given talent? Somebody's not using their God given talent(s) to the Glory of God!

One thing is for sure, you have a talent. You have a talent, I have a talent, all God's children have at least one talent. One other thing is equally true. If you don't use it, God may take it away and give it to someone else. Even if you don't think that you have a talent or you just don't know what your talent is, by all means, give to God what you know you do have. Silver and gold you may not have, but what you do have, give! Give!

It doesn't cost you any money to love God. We love Him because He first loved us.

> *Love suffers long and is kind; love does not envy; love does not parade itself, is not puffed up; does not behave rudely, does not seek its own, is not provoked, thinks no evil; does not rejoice in iniquity, but rejoices in the truth; bears all things, believes all things, hopes all things, endures all things. Love never fails...."* [1 Cor 13:4-8]

It doesn't cost you any money to have faith in the Lord. Faith can move mountains! It doesn't cost you any money to pray. Much prayer, much power, little prayer little power, no prayer, no power. It does't cost you any money to lift up the name of Jesus and praise His Holy name. When praises go up, blessings come down! Give your best to the Master. Hold up the blood stain banner of our Lord and sing:

> I'm pressing on the upward way,
> New heights I'm gaining every day;
> Still praying as I onward bound,
> Lord plant my feet on higher ground.

I want to live above the world,
Tho' Satan's darts at me are hurled;
For faith has caught a joyful sound,
The song of saints on higher ground.

I want to scale the utmost height,
And catch a gleam of glory bright;
But still I'll pray till heav'n I've found,
Lord lead me on to higher ground.

Lord, lift me up, and I shall stand
By faith, on heaven's table land;
A higher plane than I have found,
Lord, plant my feet on higher ground.
Higher Ground (Johnson Oatman, Jr.)

Chapter 4

YOU ARE IN GOD'S GENERATION

Scriptures: Psalms 90:1-11; 2 Cor. 4:1-12

Songs: 1. *Lift Him Up* (Johnson Oatman, Jr.)
2. *Am I a Soldier of the Cross?* (Isaac Watts)
3. *A Charge to Keep I Have* (Charles Wesley)
4. *If I Can Help Somebody* (A. Bazel Androzzo)

Charles Dickens, in his novel *A Tale of Two Cities*, and Houston Smith, the English poet, in his book, *Revolution in Western Thought,* might as well have been describing our generation. We are complex, in many ways, socially sophisticated, paradoxical, and even contradictory. In our society we have the very rich and the extremely poor. Our local churches, individually and collectively, are rich in material possessions and securities, yet the meaningful impact they have is apparently weak or nonexistent. In the name of peace we: bomb shoot, maim, and kill hundreds of innocent men, women, and children. We complain about the performance of our schools, yet many of us have little or no control over our own children. We eulogize the virtues of humans, yet too many of us have little, or nothing, to say about the abortion mills that murder humans before they have a chance to live. We criticize anybody and everything, nobody, I mean nobody, does it right. Yet, we often make little or no contribution to the solution. We believe that more nuclear weapons will ensure security and while you and I act out our indifferences,

Rome burns. The crime rate across the country soars. The divorce index rises. Nuclear weapons are still being bought and sold. The rich are getting more and the poor are getting less.

Despite of it all, this is an exciting time in which to live. This is still God's world. It is a great time to be alive. At the same time, never has the need for courageous, dedication been so urgent, or the opportunity to serve God been so great. It is in this context that we seek the meaning of life and the fulfillment of our own individual lives. We seek:

-Something to Live For
-Someone to Love and Someone to Love Us
-Something to Serve
-Something to Believe In and Hope For

Something to Live For

We search for something to live for. Knowing who we are and whose we are gives us a clue as to why we exist. Our reason for being is also very much tied up in our need for self-identification and self-worth. We ask the questions, "Who am I? Why was I Born? Why am I here at this location, at this time? Is this an accident or a coincidence? Does it have anything to do with my destiny? Where am I going?" Not knowing who we are or whose we are internally makes us more vulnerable to external forces that can dictate self-importance and value. Not knowing who we are or whose we are inherently contributes to a poor self-image and inferiority complex. On the contrary, the more we know about ourselves, the greater our chances are for experiencing a strong, positive, self-image, sense of self-worth, and sense of direction, purpose, and value in our lives. We search for something to live for.

Someone to Love and Someone to Love Us

To love and be loved is the craving of us all. 'Ain't no mountain high enough, ain't no valley deep enough, ain't no river wide enough, to keep me from you'. These are the words of a popular song. The thought here is simply this: there is no barrier or obstacle that can prove to be a hindrance to prevent the parties from being together. What intense determination! The reason for this conduct is easily explained. Love is as essential to life as is air and water. Without either one or the other we would surely die.

We need love, not pity or sympathy, and a lack of it leads to emotional problems, mental problems, socio-psychological problems and eventually self-destruction. We are not concerned here with mere sexual gratification, but of real concern and care. God lifted the strain and burden of anxiety and frustration from us and lightened our lives in this and other matters,

> F*or God so loved the world that he gave His only begotten Son, that whoever believes in Him should not perish but have everlasting life.* [John 3:16]

This is more fully expressed in 1 John 4:7-10, 19-20. Love is the essence of life and we will:

- climb the highest mountain
- swim the widest river
- do any and every kind of ridiculous thing

to win the love of our eye. We search for someone or something to love.

Something or Someone to Serve

Say what you will about our age. We are anxious, restless, fearful and insecure. We worry about everything, including our material possessions, our physical health, our relationships, and our money, or lack of it. There are many ways to deal with these concerns in our lives. One of these ways is through the medium of service. We need something to claim our attention, so that our talents and skills can be used and channeled into positive productive areas. Stop sitting around the house worrying, get busy doing something! We seek something or someone to serve.

The harvest is ripe, the laborers are few. The hungry and homeless are in our midst. We see them every day and ignore or pretend they don't exist. We try to pick and choose who we will, or will not work with and what causes we will, or will not support. Manytimes our efforts to serve God is regulated by convenience. For many of us, if serving God will cause a change in our normal routines, we choose not to serve. We do this at great risk to our lives and our relationship with God. We do not fully recognize nor take seriously what's involved when the scriptures teach:

> *Then He will also say to those on the left hand, "Depart from Me, you cursed, into the everlasting fire prepared for the devil and his angels: for I was hungry and you gave Me no food; I was thirsty and you gave Me no drink; I was a stranger and you did not take Me in, naked and you did not clothe Me, sick and in prison and you did not visit Me."* [Matt. 25:41-43]

> *Do not be deceived, God is not mocked; for whatever a man sows, that he will also reap.* [Gal. 6:7, cf. Matt. 25:14-30]
>
> *But I say to you that for every idle word men may speak, they will give account of it in the day of judgment.* [Matt. 12:36]

There is much work to be done. We see the need for many things we are capable of doing, but, we are hesitant about becoming personally involved. We remain unconvinced, and skeptical that our effort, our contribution will make a difference. We are not sure that our involvement will be properly recognized, or that we will be rewarded as we think we should. Sure, we see the need, and every one knows something should be done about it, but, 'Not I said the Cat.' What? Who? Me? Do That? You must be joking! Un-uhn! No way, José! Yet, we think of ourselves as loving, kind, concerned, and affectionate. Yet, for many, these noble qualities are rarely, if ever, are extended or expressed beyond the confines of our family, or a select, limited, circle of friends and/or acquaintances.

Many times our efforts are restricted and confined to those who we think will reciprocate: I'll scratch your back if you scratch mine. Our efforts are also restricted and confined to those who can satisfy our selfish motives: If I do this thing for you, what's in it for me? Faithful and obedient service to God elevates this limited, restricted view and gives us unlimited possibilities. Our service to God enlarges our perspective on life, gives character to, and deepens our commitments. It nobilizes our work. It contributes to a greater sense of self worth and value to our lives.

In life we are going to end up serving something or someone. "*...Choose for yourselves this day whom you will* *serve..."* (Josh. 24:15). Choose to serve God, from whom all blessing flow! We seek something or someone to serve.

Something to Believe in and Hope For

Belief in God eliminates anxiety, despair and hopelessness. When all else fails, when everything that seems so right goes very wrong, hope arrives and it is our last attempt to grasp on and hold on to something. After all is said and done, hope emerges as the life sustaining force working in our lives. That is what is being expressed in this song:

When peace like a river, attendeth my way
When sorrow like sea billows roll;
What ever my lot,
Thou hast taught me to say,
It is well, it is well with my soul

It is well- with my soul-
It is well, it is well with my soul.
It is Well with My Soul (H. G. Spafford)

And in this, no greater sense of security can be found.

Knowing who we are in Christ together with our belief in God completely satisfies our need to place our hope in something and also makes our need to serve joyous, not burdensome.

One scripture indicates that we spend our lives as a tale, a living epistle that is told (2 Cor. 3:2,3). What an observation! This suggest that as we think back and reflect upon our lives and our experiences, there are so many aspects of them, so many good things that has happened, we can't fully explain why they happened to us. It seems like a fairy tale! By all accounts, by every indicator, and not even by stretching our wildest imagination can we fully explain why we, as individuals and as a people, give an account for our present circumstances. It all seems so unreal, so unbelievable.

According to some people, Blacks were not supposed to be considered human beings. By others, Blacks were thought to be incapable of learning and deserved no formal education. We had no money, no power (from a sociopolitical perspective), and little or no influence or authority. Except for those nineteen Negroes who came to this country (Jamestown) as indentured servants in 1619, along with others who had a similar status, the remainder of us were brought to this and other parts of the world not of our own choice, but as slaves. We were told that we were pre-destined to be hewers of wood, and drawers of water. We had no rights or privileges a White man was obligated to honor or respect. And because we were so brainwashed, many of us accepted this decree (affecting a whole people) with little or no questions asked. Many of the vicissitudes of that time remain today.

Yet, today, not because of the situation, but despite of it, we stand in some of the highest places in some of the land. We have, all too often, underestimated our own God-given skills and abilities. Furthermore, we have not set our goals high enough and have been too eager to be satisfied with second best. We have also allowed others to dictate the do and don't, the can and the can not of our lives, while at the same time, God's command to subdue and have dominion over all the earth, the fish of the seas and the fouls of the air applies. If it had not been for the Lord on my side, where would we Be? It is important and meaningful to look back and wonder how we got over.

It was the Lord who created you and I in His image and likeness. To this one writer exclaimed,

> *Behold what manner of love the Father has bestowed on us, that we should be called children of God!...* [1 John 3:1]

It was the Lord who put clapping in our hands, dancing in our feet, and joy in our hearts. It was the Lord that caused us to have the peace that passes all understanding, that causes us to have faith in the midst of despairing situations. This is why our hope is built upon nothing less than Jesus' blood and righteousness. We dare not trust the sweetest frame, but wholly lean on Jesus' name. All other ground is sinking sand. We know that all good-byes aren't for good. We know that all sicknesses are not unto death. We believe, and indeed, know that the Lord has not brought us this far to leave us. We know that weeping may endure for a night, but joy comes in the morning. We have come this far by faith, leaning on the Lord, trusting in His holy word. He has never failed us yet. It is my prayerful hope that we do not fail to understand what that means, and by no means forget it.

God's Generation

What does it mean, that this is God's Generation? Does this indicate that the everlasting God, who changes not, was not the God of previous generations? God forbid! The scripture for this occasion makes it abundantly clear, that this is not the case, *"Lord, You have been our dwelling place in all generations"* (Ps. 90:1). What then, is so unique, so different, so distinctive, about this one?

First of all, you are in it. We may read, discuss, theorize, speculate, or whatever, about what did, or did not happen. We were not there, none of us was on the scene. Secondly, God is dealing with you and I in a somewhat different and special way than he did with other generations.

We must keep in mind, that it was through great trials and tribulations, toils and snares, through much heartaches, suffering, agony and humiliation that our forefathers, and believers through the ages, have bequeathed to us, this generation, a legacy more precious than gold. They have, through great sacrifices and diligence, provided us (you and I), with the real opportunity (not guarantee) to stand up and be counted as free men and women - as God intended.

No longer are we hindered, or bounded by the tradition of the capricious demands of slave masters, those who hampered, and thwarted our efforts to be what God intended us to be. No longer are we intimidated by the threats of people afflicted with the delusion of racial, moral, or intellectual superiority. "Stony the road we trod, bitter the chastening rod..." *Lift Every Voice and Sing* (James Weldon Johnson). Yet, and despite of and through it all, we have arrived on the stages of history - we remain in the land of the living and never has the time been so right for us to stand up and be counted. We must not forget: if we can see further, or understand more fully; if we dare to be bold, confident, even over-confident, - it is because we stand on the shoulders of many great, dedicated men and women who bored their burdens in the heat of the day, who ran and did not get tired, who walked and did not faint, who did not get weary in well-doing.

Because of these valiant, courageous, and steadfast efforts, it can be safely said, "Never in history of the world, has so much been given to so many, for so little in return by so few." Many of us take so much for granted.

Even more, by the time you and I were born:

- The forest had been cleared.

- The railroad had been built.
- Schools were erected.
- Roads and bridges were charted out.
- Telephone and power lines were laid
- Radio and T.V. were common place.

This and a host and variety of things we take for granted. With all this before us, keep in mind that the challenges to this generation remain the same as ever. The hopes, the aims, and the aspirations of men and women the world over, are unchanged. We still need and long for:

-Something to Live For
-Someone to Love and Someone to Love Us
-Something to Serve
-Something to Believe In and Hope For

We, you and I, are co-workers with the eternal God, our Father and creator of the universe. No greater challenge or partnership can be dreamed of, or imagined. What an honor!! What a privilege!! What more could one ask for.

Finally, let me remind you that all Believers (in God) throughout the ages have experienced problems peculiar to their times. Moses, that great patriarch of the Old Testament, had to deal with the unbelieving, stubborn, reluctant, Pharaoh. The prophets, Isaiah, Jeremiah, Ezekiel, Elijha,... had to contend with all sorts of superstitions and weird religious practices. Jesus had to face the antagonism of sectarian, orthodox, traditional Jewish sects. This, together with superstition, was also one of Paul's real concerns -- as pointed out in our text. The Reformation Believers (Luther, Calvin,...) surely all had their problems.

Are we today any different? No! No! No! We have many of the same problems and more. We, in the church, have to deal with the modern, sophisticated, radical, liberated woman and the deluded, so-called highly educated, independent self-made man. This, while it is possible, is no easy task. We are living in a different time, things have changed. We don't do that anymore. Or, that is not the way it use to be done. To be sure, there is some merit in that argument, but it is also part of the problem. We all have changed, grown older, and, hopefully, wiser. This church is not the same today as it was on yesterday. Members have come and some have gone. The pastor is not the same. He is older, wiser, and, pray to God, more spiritual. This city and community try to make it clear that it is on the move, but, like so many other aspects of life, it is only one side of a picture or story we want others to see or hear. There is much physical misery of one kind or another and spiritual blindness. This means there is much work to be done.

Does anyone believe that the only reason why this church facility is here at this location is because the Lord God of this universe had no other location or place to put a church? The answer is obviously no. This church facility and the members of this body of Christ are here for a reason, a special reason, and that is to hold up the blood-stained banner of our Lord, and to herald the riches of the Gospel.

As you think of the blessings God has bestowed upon you and your family, where God has brought you from, and His continued protection and guidance afforded to you, what will be the legacy you leave to your children and the next generation? As you ponder this question keep in mind you are still the light of the world. You are still the salt of the earth. No matter who, or how they try to deny it, the world is still hungry for the Living Bread and it is our job to lift the Savior up for them to see. Jesus said, *"And I, if I am lifted up from the earth, will draw all peoples to Myself"* (John 12:32). Remember our text,

> *...If our gospel be veiled, it is veiled to those that are perishing, whose minds the god of this age has blinded, who do not believe, lest the light of the gospel of the glory of Christ, who is the image of God, should shine on them.* [2 Cor. 4:3-4]

Satan is still alive and well. He is going to and fro to see who he may devour (1 Peter 5:8). Sinners and skeptics are bountiful. The harvest is ripe. The laborers are few. The need is apparent. The challenge is clear. Remember, we are the light of the world, the salt of the earth. We must let our light shine.

Am I a soldier of the cross?
A foll'wer of the lamb?
And shall I fear to own His cause
Or blush to speak His name?
Must I be carried to the skies
On flow'ry beds of ease,
While others fought to win the prize
And sailed thru bloody seas?
Am I a Soldier of the Cross? (Issac Watts)

A charge to keep I have,
a God to Glorify,
Who gave His son my soul to save,
And fit it for the sky.
A Charge to Keep I Have (Charles Wesley)

If I can help somebody
as I pass along,
If I can cheer somebody
with a word or song,

If I can show somebody
He is traveling wrong
Then my living shall not be in vain.

If I can point somebody
to the Lamb once slain
If I can tell somebody
that He rose again
That He can cleanse the guilty,
He can wash the stain
Then my living shall not be in vain.
If I Can Help Somebody
(A. Bazel Androzzo)

Chapter 5

THE GOD WHO GAMBLES

Scriptures: Job 1:1-22; 2:1-10; 42:1-17

Songs: 1. *Count on Me* (E.E. Hewitt)
2. *Lead Me, Guide Me* (Doris Akers)
3. *O Jesus I Have Promise* (John E. Bode)

Perhaps, you may wonder, and rightly so, what this preacher has in mind when referring to God as a gambler. Is this some kind of joke? What is going on here? Surely, gambling is not one of the characteristics of God you have been taught, and have come to believe and know of Him. One thing is for sure, I better hurry up and explain myself before I get thrown out of this pulpit and out of this church, and fast! I'm sure you do not put up with such hum-bug foolishness.

In the first place, some may think, I can not even imagine why God needs to gamble or even want to. He owns everything, or so He claims. So Rev. Johnson, let's get on with it. We are anxiously awaiting what you have to say about this matter, and it better be good, and it better be quick!

Come on Rev. Johnson, since we know a little bit about you, we are going to give you a break, and ask you nicely and politely, are you serious about what you said about God and gambling? Come on, be for real. Are you referring to the God of Abraham, Isaac, and Jacob? Is the God you are referring to the creator of heaven and earth? Is this God the father of our Lord and Savior Jesus Christ? I respect your right to know the answer to these questions and others as well. Thank you for your questions. Now here is my answer. The answer to every question is: yes, yes, yes!

I meant everything exactly as the subject says or implies. Anthropomorphically speaking, God did, in the language of the scripture for today, gamble. Anthropomorphism is the act of attributing human shape or characteristics to a god, an animal, or an inanimate thing. Often this is necessary in order for man, who is carnal and finite in nature, to understand various truths pertaining to Jehovah, the God of Abraham, Isaac, and Jacob, who is a spirit and is infinite in nature. Look at the scripture found in Job 1:6-12.

God gambled on the integrity of a man called Job. To gamble means to take a risk. The gambler may win or he may lose. There is no guarantee the gambler will either win or lose. Satan made a bet with God that the integrity of Job and his commitment to his belief, could not stand the mighty onslaught which he, the devil could and would pit against him. The deal was on. Now, all we have to do is wait for the outcome. Understand this, Job, like you and me, was born with a free will. God created us all with a free will. He has provided us with the freedom to choose, whether to serve Him or not.

In the scripture there is a conversation between God and satan. Satan explains to God that he had been going to and fro in the land, devouring all he had come into contact with. The impression Satan was trying to give was that everyone he met was either a cream puff or a pushover. He was boasting about his many victories and gloating over his success. God called satan's attention to Job. Satan's attitude regarding Job was that Job would present no difficult challenge.

Satan pointed out the reason why he thought Job served God in the first place. After all, Job was not only rich, but he was very rich. So Job's reason or motive was brought into consideration. Why is Job serving you? Why is his allegiance to you so strong? *"...Does Job fear God for nothing"* (Job 1:9)? He has a vested interest in serving you. Confident of victory, satan said, I'll bet You that if You take away the prosperity You have surrounded him with, *"...he will surely curse You to Your face"* (Job 1:11)! God's response was, you're on!

Soon after the bet was confirmed Job began to experience a series of major disasters which could have, and did affect his life. Job was told by the only survivor that all of his oxen and asses, servants included, had been taken away by the Sabeans (Job 1:13-15). Even while Job was being given this information, another servant came and told him fire had destroyed all his sheep and servants (Job 1:16). In the presence of these two bearers of bad news came still another messenger with more horrible tales. The Chaldeans, made up of three bands, took away Job's camels (Job 1:17). While these were talking still more horrible stories arrived. Job's sons and daughters had been killed in a hurricane (Job 1:18-19). Later, Job's body was so disfigured by sores, his closest friends could hardly recognize him. In this context Job suffered and suffered much. We have come to know Job because of his suffering.

While it is true, and also proper to point out, and emphasize the suffering plight of Job, we must not lose sight of, and also keep in focus what could be considered the most crucial aspect of this book. I believe it is given to us in the second chapter, verse nine. *"Then his wife said to him, 'Do you still hold to your integrity? Curse God and die'"* (Job 2:9)! You see brothers and sisters, ladies and gentlemen, this book deals primarily with integrity, a character trait we often hear about but rarely see. Integrity, that is what this message is about. Integrity, not suffering!

You mean to tell me all of the misfortune God has allowed to be your lot, you are still singing and worshipping his name? What kind of man are you? What kind of God would do such a thing? Why don't you just curse God and die? *"...You speak as one of the foolish women speaks..."* (Job 2:10). How many of us here today would have the same or similar response? Let something tragic happen to us or someone we know and watch us question, blame, and even curse God! You took my mother from me! Curse. My daddy molested me! Curse. I got laid off! I got fired! Curse, curse. My car broke down and I don't have the money to get it fixed. Curse, curse, curse.

Integrity is a character trait. It is a part of one's personality. It is a very fruitful word which involves not only what a person thinks of himself or herself, but about God, about his neighbor, about his environment. Integrity means wholeness, completeness, fullness, unity, soundness. Most of all, it means honesty. Yes, even faithfulness and dependability. All these wonderful features are involved in, and constitute a vital aspect of such a rich word.

Satan, I have confidence in this man whose name is Job. Just do not do him any physical harm. The rest is left up to you and your heinous, ingenious imagination. Satan accepted the terms and went to work immediately. There was no turning back.

Quite often it does not take much to make us go off, or charge God foolishly. The least little thing that happens to us or to someone we know, we get upset. For example, I won't sing in the choir. I'll show him, I'll just sit out here and watch. That is, if I go back to church at all. I won't sit on the deacon board, I won't sit on the trustee board, I won't participate in the singles ministry, I won't usher, I won't do this and I won't do that because I don't like the way they make decisions, or do things. We blame God for every misfortune that befalls us and charge Him foolishly. We become bitter, arrogant, disrespectful, resentful, unbelieving.

God is gambling that young men and women, boys and girls, especially those who claim to be Christians, will have the courage and integrity to stand up, to do the right thing, and all that is pleasing and acceptable in His sight. God is gambling that ministers who claim to be representatives of the Lord and Savior Jesus Christ, will not be chicken, or timid cowards in their presentation of the gospel, but will preach with conviction, boldness, and power, as they contend for the faith once delivered unto the saints, no matter what the world may or may not do. Customs may change, traditions may vary, heartaches, troubles, sickness, pain, and even death may be our lot. Will we charge God foolishly or will we be able to say, " Through it all I've learned to trust in Jesus, I've learn to trust in God!" Will we be able to sing, "Whatever my lot, Thou has taught me to say, it is well, it is well, with my soul?" Will we be able to boldly proclaim, "The Lord giveth and the Lord taketh away, blessed be the name of the Lord?"

Does the choir, the deacon board, the usher board, the preachers, the trustee board, the members of this church have integrity? Have you been faithful and obedient to God? Can God depend on you? God is gambling with satan that you will get your act together and prove again what everybody already knows, satan is a liar and a looser. Always has been, and always will be. Whenever and wherever he has the gall or audacity to challenge not only God, but God's people, his fate has already been determined.

You may recall, that at the beginning of our scripture reading Job was not only rich, but very rich. The richest man in the land, in a material sense. He had a lovely family, his daughters were the fairest in the land. This tells us that his wife must have been a very beautiful woman. Did Job's stubborn, tenacious cling to his belief in God gain him anything? You bet it did! God is faithful to those who trust in him. You can be assured that if the Lord tells you or I something through His word, you can depend on it. There is no element of chance, no ifs, ands or buts. No risk. No gamble. Just assurance.

Integrity has its rewards. So Job did not curse God and die. Big deal. What did he get out of it? Job did not succumb to the temptation to go along with popular opinion. You know the idea that says, "To get along, you have to go along." In every walk of life, business, industry, art, music, in every area of life one popular notion or idea is, "Don't rock the boat." Another popular idea is, "If you can't beat them, join them." Why not, "Become one of the boys or a part of the 'In' crowd?" Those individuals who decide to be different, or do otherwise are the exception, not the rule. They don't settle for less. They rise above the rest, above the level of mediocrity. They are true champions. Warriors in the army of the Lord. Defenders of truth and the faith!

I am preaching and teaching about Job because he was the exception, a true champion. Curse God and die? Woman, you talk so foolish! All of my appointed days will I wait until my change comes. God has not brought me this far to leave me. He who has begun a work in us will perfect it until the coming of the Lord (Phil. 1:6). Lord help me to hold out, until my change comes.

Knowing the outcome and implications of God's decision to accept the challenge, God was not about to let Job be put into a position that would cast disbelief in the loving and caring God we have come to know. Job's position was a clinch to win. A hands down, automatic victory. God was not then and is not now going to allow his faithful children, who desire to do his will, to be put into a trick bag by the cunning, craftiness of satan. God will not permit us to be tempted beyond what we are able to bear (1 Cor. 10:13).The truth of the matter is, satan tied the rope around his own neck when he made the challenge. God knew what the outcome would be. God is omnipotent (all powerful) and omniscient (all knowing). Satan in his feeble attempt to destroy Job, actually caused Job to be blessed! Since Job came through so beautifully, and with flying colors, how could God do anything less than give proper reward to the faithful? God richly rewarded Job. He got double for all of his material possessions, more children , and a long life. Will God do anything different for you if you are faithful. If satan is attacking you, start rejoicing now for victory is yours. Victory is guaranteed in the name of Jesus! Hallelujah! God will bless you for your victory! Continue to be faithful. Job is our example of what God did do and will do for all who trust in Him. As the song states:

When we walk with the Lord
In the light of His Word,
What a glory He sheds on our way!
While we do His good will
He abides with us still,
And with all who will trust and obey.

Trust and obey - For there's no other way
To be happy in Jesus But to trust and obey.
Trust and Obey (John H. Sammis)

This story of Job tells us that if we hold up our heads and do not bow to the temptation to compromise our integrity and maintain our high ethical, moral, and religious, principles, God will grant us the victory, the success you seek, and the desires of your heart. On the flip side, it should come as no surprise that those who involve themselves in any kind of mischievous, conniving, cunning, scam, scheme or plot against a child of God or are involved in any way in any thing harmful or damaging to a true child of God, they will not only fail, as did satan, but effect the opposite result they sought! God is all wise and all powerful and cares for His children so much that gave His only begotten Son to die for our sins. God will not permit satan to prosper over those who love the Lord and are faithful to Him. Weeping may endure for a night but joy will come in the morning.

We need to be very careful how we conduct ourselves, especially if we call, or consider ourselves Christians, or children of God. Remember, we are held by God to have a different, higher, but fair standard in all we do. God's expectation of us is not the same for everyone. Remember, this message is not simply about Job but more importantly about integrity, honesty, faithfulness, and accountability. God accepted a bet from satan, God is gambling that men and women, boys and girls, mothers and fathers, will not only face the many challenges and temptations of all sorts but be victorious in their efforts to glorify Him. Though you may be persecuted, will you join in with Job and say, *"I will wait till my change comes"* (Job 14:14)? You must remember that it pays to serve Jesus. If you continue in the faith once delivered unto the saints, the Lord will fight your battles and victory will be yours in Christ Jesus. You can point to Job and say, look what happened to him, how awful, how sad. But you can also say look what a mighty God did for him who believed and trusted in God. A finer example you cannot find than in the life of Job.

With that in mind, would the Lord gamble with satan regarding your integrity? When you first met the Lord, what promises did you make with God if he freed your soul from the gates of hell? Do you remember what that promise was? Did you make one? What did the Lord say to you through His word that He would do if you took Him at His word, and stand on His promises? Can God depend upon you? Can God count on you?

The Lord has need of workers,
to till His field today,
So kindly He has led me
to walk in wisdom's way;
I pray for grace to help me
with all my heart to say,
O blessed Savior, count on me.

Now gird me for the battle
when evil pow'rs oppose,
And give me faith and courage
to conquer o'er Thy foes;
I pledge Thee my allegiance,
my soul no other knows,
O blessed Savior, count on me.

Count on me, count on me,
For loving hearted service glad and free;
Yes, count on me, count on me,
O blessed Savior, count on me.
Count on Me (E. E. Hewitt)

Chapter 6

TOO MUCH, TOO LITTLE, TOO LATE

Scripture: John 3:16-17; I John 4:10-19; Rom. 8:35,38,39

Songs: 1. *Jesus Loves Me* (William B. Bradbury)
2. *Come to Jesus* (unknown)
3. *Love Lifted Me* (James Rowe)

Perhaps there is no way to verify this observation, but I venture this thought, with respect to music and love, more than 85% of all music deals with L O V E -- love. This theme can be divided into three broad categories. The first of these deal with happiness. I found my baby! My baby Loves me! It's an enjoyable, thrilling, experience. The second major theme deals with the unhappy, the sad. The blues. I lost my baby. The words and tune may vary, but, the theme is the same, I'm broken hearted and sad. The third category has to do with that group of people who have neither lost or found their baby -- they're still looking. I do not know who's the worst off. Those who lost their baby, or those who can not find their baby.

At any rate, love has a way of playing psychological tricks on us. It makes an old man and woman think they are younger than they are and it tends to make the young man and woman think they are older and more mature than they are. Neither group is the wiser. Most all of the secular music written is a variation on the theme of love. The same pervasive theme of love prevails in sacred music.

Because of love men and women have respect for themselves and others. The presence of love causes men and women to marry, stay with their spouse for riches or poor, in sickness and in health 'til death do them part. Because of love men sail the mighty oceans, swim in raging waters, climb rugged mountains, and work two or more jobs to provide for their families. Love is a motivating force for good in this world. In fact, it is the motivating force that rescues men and women, boys and girls from sin and death. God understands this. He knows that if men and women do not commit themselves to love and direct this love correctly, they would be doomed to death and destruction.

The reason for the universal, pervasive and persistent focus on the theme of love is simple. Love is as essential to life as is air and water. Our lives, our very existence depends upon loving and being genuinely loved by someone. Satan, our adversary, the great deceiver knows this. His job is to make you fall in love with the wrong thing or person and get you to believe no one genuinely loves you. Who or what are you in love with? Do you believe that someone genuinely loves you for who you are? That's a question you need to think about today.

To live in a world with the thought, or idea that no one is interested in you or no one cares about you is distressful, anxiety producing, a natural disaster, a beautiful creation on its way to death and destruction, a ticking time bomb, an accident waiting to happen, a sad story without a happy ending, a deception, a lie, a tragedy!

What I have in mind is a honest, caring, genuine, concern on the part of one person or group that is not confined to one's self, one's individual family, circle of friends, and/or associates. If Love is not of this dimension and quality, it is open to question. The motive for action is questionable. God knows we have a need to be cared for. For without it our lives would be filled with apprehension, hopelessness and anxiety. Knowing that someone is concerned and cares provides the basis upon which the foundation of the Christian hope rests. To know that someone cares removes the unneeded burden of worry about this or that, or, whatever. It allows us to have confidence in ourselves and in our ability to live out our lives. We face each day with the assured confidence that the next will be brighter and better.

With the confident assurance that someone cares enough to love us, we can be more relaxed, psychologically, and emotionally calm. We can perform our duties and responsibilities; arduous and difficult, as they may be, with the knowledge and confidence we are more than equal to the challenges that lie before and around us. This is the basis upon which we make such outlandish, ridiculous assertions such as this wild claim:

> Ain't no mountain high enough,
> and no valley deep enough
> to keep me from you.

But this unabashed confidence can and do apply to other areas of life as well.

Just like the positive features of love do so much to enhance the quality and stability of our lives, the opposite, or absence of love, or the belief, real or imagined, that no one cares, no one loves us has some very devastating, negative, consequences upon our lives. In turn we become nervous, unstable, and neurotic. We become disorganized, disoriented, disinterested, lackadaisical, and indifferent, which often is to the detriment of ourselves and to those around us. Consider the drama of young lovers.

Young Lovers

They're young, energetic, excited, and so they thought, in love. Their relationship has been going on for sometime. Everything seems to be going along well. They even have thoughts of going down the aisle, but, suddenly, there is a break in this wonderful promising relationship. The young lovers have a parting of the ways.

What happened? What went wrong? How could an association like theirs, which started out so nice, end up like this? What caused this relationship, that seemed so promising, that seemed so right, to turn out to be so wrong? Surely he must have done something obnoxious and dumb that turned her away, something she could take no more. To him, he still has not come to grip with this situation. The reality of this situation seems so unreal. He says to himself, "Am I dreaming? I'm confused. Am I missing something?" He still can't believe what's happening. All he knows is that he has an undesirable situation on his hand. Oh how he wishes it would just go away.

He remembered the many times when a two-bit ice cream soda, had the same value as an expensive dinner, with all the trimmings. There was never a time when he had to go out of his way to prove anything. At that time, it was the thought that mattered. Now, with the threat of a possible break-up on his mind, my man decides he must do something to prove himself to her. He is now nervous, uneasy, and filled with apprehension coupled with anxiety. He had never felt this way before. All the other times he was confident and sure. He keeps telling himself, "This is so unreal."

This is not the way things were suppose to be. After all, didn't he brag about being a lady killer? How many times had he boasted about his magnificent personality and his irresistible charm. As he would have the boys, and anybody else who cared to know, he personified what every beautiful girl dreamed of, to say nothing of the more homely and not so beautiful crowd.

As much as he tried, he couldn't shake that nervous feeling, in spite of all the precautions and care he had given to this all important mission. To win the heart of his sweet-heart, he took a real bath. Not the usual, hurry-up wash cloth routine. He used water, hot water, as hot as he could stand. He used real soap. Plenty of it. He stayed in the shower a long time. After that he bought some 'High Karate'. To that he added a hefty dose of 'Brute', capped off by some 'Old Spice'. He got himself smelling almost like a 'sissy'. He brushed his teeth for a long time. When that was done, he washed his mouth with 'Listerine' and 'Scope', topped off with two 'Clorets'. My man took no chances! His suit was cleaned and pressed. His shoes were shined. His suite, tie, and shoes all were in impeccable order. He was clean, squeaky clean!

Never before in his life had he felt as he did now. Not only was he nervous, he was almost scared. He felt as he had never felt before. If anybody wanted things to go right, if ever there was a time when he wanted not to make even the slightest mistake, it was now. Still he was both nervous and determined. He decided to go for broke -- let it all hang out. But, he wasn't apologizing to anyone. He didn't care how much it would cost. He just wanted to be in the good graces of his lady. What ever it cost to gain that without losing his manhood and his pride, he would gladly pay it eagerly .

He arrived at dream girl's house in a stretch limousine (big bucks!) with two dozen long stemmed roses (Mo' money!) and some expensive perfume (Mo' money!). He had gotten the word that the lady likes candy so, you guessed it, he had that, too (Mo' money!). He finally got up the nerve to ring the bell. In what seemed to be an eternity of waiting, he rang the bell again. There are times in our lives when one minuet seems like an hour, or forever, this was one of those times for lover boy -- the lady killer. Finally, the door opened and there she was. The most beautiful woman in the world, or so he thought. She was all decked out in a dingy looking well-worn petty coat. Her hair was going all over the place, even with all of the curlers decorating her head. All in all, on this occasion, she was a sight for sore eyes. You know how the real thing can look, without cosmetics and other beauty enhancers.

After a moment the goddess spoke, "What do you want? What are you doing here?" He says to himself, what is wrong with this woman? What does she mean what do I want? She should know. Doesn't she see me with all these goodies: flowers, candy, perfume? Doesn't she realize how much all this stuff cost? What is her problem? If she thinks I'm going to apologize, she is out of her mind!

Well, to make a long story short, this proved to be the worse day of his life. Never had he experienced anything like this before. He had heard about the fury of a woman. Now, he had first hand experience, in the worst kind of way. He was crushed.

A man not given to strong drink, he heard how some people drown out their troubles by drinking. What the heck, he thought, nothing to lose. I'll give it a try. For the bartender, this is an every day, common experience. He knows what to do about it. The bartender psyched lover boy into believing that he was given the strongest drink in the house when in fact the opposite was true. Lover boy had been given two drinks, one with coke-a-cola and seltzer water, the other seven-up with some ginger ale and an olive. There was absolutely no liquor in either drink, but that is not what lover boy thought. He had never been drunk before. Now he thinks he is drunk. In this frame of mind, he stumbles over to one of the nearest seats to wallow in his misery and ponder his woes.

What happened? What went wrong? As he sat down he wondered what did he do, or did not do, to deserve this kind of treatment. For the life of him, he could come up with no satisfactory answer. Yet, his crime was so obvious and blatant. While lover boy was pondering the situation, a couple of fellows happened to pass by. Said one to the other, "Hey man, isn't that lover boy over there? What's he doing here?"

"Come on man, get real. Haven't you heard?"

"Heard what?"

"Lover boy got dumped!"

"What? You got to be joking."

"No, I am not. Trust me."

"Wow! You just wait until I tell the fellows about this!"

Drowsy, slightly dazed, but in a fair state of mind, lover boy over heard the brothers, jumped up and screamed, how did they know? That poor fellow, any other time a question like that would never enter his mind. He knew the answer. They got it through the 'Grape Vine'. Every body knows the fastest mode of communication is the 'Grape Vine'. The vine is faster than the telephone and faster than the telegraph. He thought, and thought, and thought. Then said to himself, "I should have just apologized, even though I'm not exactly clear as to what I did that was so wrong. The first words out of my mouth should have been, 'I'm sorry. I blew it! I Love you'. Oh God, I really do love her."

Meanwhile, lover girl has a conversation with her friend. Girl, guess who came over to my house? That's right, mister *lover boy*. Girl, I could hardly believe my eyes. I don't know what he did, but he was looking good. He almost swept me off my feet! You talk about looking sharp, that man was looking so good, I started to grab him and hug him like a teddy bear and squeeze him tight. Then I caught myself. I put my hands on my hips and I went off. Yes I did. I was all over him. I let him have it, with both barrels, just like you said I should do. I really socked it to him.

After a few more calls, as she sits in her room, she becomes very solemn and an atmosphere of sadness prevails. Before long lover girl is crying. She drys her eyes and then crys some more, and more, and more. She thinks to herself and comes to the conclusion, that she really does like old lover boy after all, in a serious way. He was a real nice guy most of the time, a real gentleman some of the time, and he did treat her with respect all the time.

She recalls how her girl friends told her all the horror stories about boys and how she made up her mind that she would not put up with any mess from any guy. Then she met lover boy. Oh, her girl friends were so jealous. He was so different from all the rest. So different from what she had heard about him. Yes, she even admitted falling in love with him. Now she is upset because she listened to her friends and came down too hard on the brother and fears they won't be getting back together. She feels she demanded too much, she showed too little understanding, compassion patience, and forgiveness, and now its too late.

A little later some friends came to lover girl's house. They learned that lover girl had been crying, and hard! "What's the matter?" someone asked. Someone told the story. They talked discovered that lover girl really loved lover boy and wanted to marry him. Someone cried, "What? I don't believe this! You mean she is crying because of that no good bum?" Someone else cried, "I told you, I told you." "Girlfriend, I ain't in it! I ain't in it. Out'da here. I'm out'a here!"

Lover boy's problem was that he tried to do too much all at once. Flowers, perfume, and candy are lovely gifts for ladies, given under the right circumstances. In lover boy's case, an attempt was made to give his lovely lady these gifts, but having taken her for granted for so long, this last minute, frantic, desperate act of adoration and appreciation proved to be too much, too late. For you see, he took her for granted much too long. During the time they were together there was too little appreciation he showed her. And now it was too late to make up for it.

Taking anyone or anything for granted too long carries negative consequences. Deep seeded feelings of resentment, hurt, anger, and hate will be expressed in various ways and at the same time love will become suppressed. Before long Love will say, "I can't live here no more." This is not only true for couples and marriages which are personal relationships, but applies to professional relationships, inter office relationships, church leadership relationships, cultural relationships, relationships between different generations, etc. Too much bad coupled with too little good can lead to situations where it is too late for any hope restoration.

Anyway, back to the young lovers. What we have here are two people in love, separated from each other because of a bunch of foolishness. It's a mess. Oh, it could be worked out with proper communication. Will it get worked out? Who knows.

How is God's love and our relationship with God different? Despite what has been said, a good, loving God who does all things well, continues to shower us with numerous untold blessings. He is still giving sight to the blind and hope to the downcast, depressed and oppressed. He is still a mother to the motherless, a father to the fatherless, he is still the Great Physician, giving healing power to the hurt and sickly, food to the homeless and hungry, joy to the humble and lowly, and strength to the weary and fainthearted. It doesn't matter who is in the White House, God is still on the throne.

It is both ironic and a tragedy that this man who put forth his best effort, who spared nothing to gain the love and fellowship of the one whose affection he so desperately wanted, even needed, was not able to state his case, or explain his motives. He spared nothing. He let it all hang out. Despite this, he was humiliated and insulted. His best effort was futile. This could never have happened had he come to God. How different the situation would have been; no worries or anguishing moments about the 'Grape Vine', or peer pressure. *"...The one who comes to Me I will by no means cast out "* (John 6:37).

When you come to the Lord, you do not have to be concerned with cosmetics, how you look or what you should wear. He made you and knows all about you, even the contents of your mind. A rush job done in haste and panic will in no way make an impression. Just as the sister saw through the thin veneer of a shallow commitment -- God sees through shallow commitments and superficial attempts to please Him. Even our so-called righteousness is as filthy rags before God (Is. 64:6). The real you is who God is concerned with, not with the outward you. He is concerned with your thoughts, your motives, and your feelings. This is why Proverbs 4:23 is so important, *"Keep your heart with all diligence for out of it spring the issues of life."*

Unlike with the young lovers, with God, its never a situation of too much, too little too late. Maybe you feel you've taken God for granted too long. Maybe you feel there has been too much bad in your life, too little good in your life and now its too late to get right with God. Maybe you feel God won't accept you the way you are now. Maybe you fell you must get yourself all fixed up before approaching God for help. If you feel it's too late to salvage your relationship with God, your wrong! God loves you and invites you to come to Him just as you are. Jesus says,

> *Behold, I stand at the door and knock. If anyone hears My voice and opens the door, I will come in to him and dine with him, and he with Me.* [Rev. 3:20]

Its not too late. If you can hear the sound of my voice, it's not too late. Come to Jesus now. The sun may be going down, but it's not too late. Come to Jesus, come to Jesus, come to Jesus just now. Too much -- this may be true. Too little -- this may be true, too. But it's never too late. Praise God, it's not too late. Come to Jesus, just now. He will save you, He will forgive you, He will cleanse you, He is able, He is willing, Jesus loves you, only trust Him. Come, He invites you to restore your relationship with Him today. Right now. Come, it's not too late.

Chapter 7

WHAT ON EARTH IS GOD DOING?

Scripture: 1 Cor. 3:9; 2 Tim. 2:11-13

Song: 1. *Make Me A Blessing* (Ira B. Wilson)

> My goodness gracious alive! What in the world are you doing back there? Come here where I can see you. I have to keep my eyes on you. I want to see you at all times. I want to know what you are doing -- what you are up to.

Then when you don't see or hear anything you say, "Things are too quiet. I wonder what he or she is up to now?"

Unlike a situation like this, we are well aware of the situation in our city, country, and around the world.

-People are still fighting and killing one another.

-Our jails are overcrowded with people who may or may not be guilty of one crime or another.

-Divorce and family problems are no longer the exception. They are a way of life.

-Teenage pregnancy is common place. It's not noticed anymore.

-Illegal drugs has become a multi-billion dollar enterprise that no one is able to extinquish.

-And God knows there is confusion and dissension in our churches all over this land.

Don't you ever wonder where God is and what He is doing about these situations?

God is showering manifold blessings upon His children, both here in this place where you are now located and countless other places around the world on this good earth.

You woke up this morning from last night's sleep to the light of another new day. You took it for granted because it has happened so often in the past you just knew tomorrow was guaranteed. All you had to do was claim it and be on your way, involving yourself in the daily routine or activities of your choice.

You have eyes that see. So what? What's the big deal there? Doesn't everyone have eyes? We were born with them true enough. But, what about The Lighthouse Inc.? What's this non-profit vision rehabilitation agency about?

You have ears that hear. You bet I do, so what? Have you ever heard of the Hearing Aid Society? No? Count your blessings. Some people have ears but cannot hear.

Have you ever heard of mental illness? You haven't? Well I have a 25-year-old niece with the mind of a 2-year-old. If your mental status is good, count it, you are blessed.

What our biggest problem is you don't know what to wear to church or work, or where ever, think about the people who don't have clothes. Count your blessings, they're from God. Another big problem of yours is that you wish the preacher would hurry up, sit down, and shut his mouth. Still another big problem is being tired and having to go to work. Boy! What a problem! What a predicament! Have you heard what the latest unemployment figures are? You have a job? It is a blessing from God! Count it.

In our homes, in our schools, in our churches, on our jobs or at play, God is blessing us. If we would stop complaining and count out blessings, it might surprise you to see what God has and continues to do for us.

> Count your blessings,
> name them one by one;
> Count your blessings,
> see what God hath done.
> Count your blessings,
> name them one by one;
> Count your blessings,
> see what God hath done.
> *Count your Blessings* (Johnson Oatman, Jr.)

God is inspiring and encouraging people to do his will. God has set before us a very tantalizing proposition for consideration. God's word states,

> *If my people who are called by my name will humble themselves, and pray and seek My face, and turn from their wicked ways, then I will hear from heaven, and will forgive their sin and heal their land.* [2 Chr. 7:14]

In this text, the blessings are conditional. We are dealing with an "if/then" situation, i.e., if you do this, then God will do that. If you don't do this, then God is not obligated to do that.

The writer David wrote,

> *I have been young, and now am old; Yet I have not seen the righteous forsaken, Nor his descendants begging bread.* [Ps. 37:25]

You are a child of God. You got a problem? You got a concern? You got a question? Take it to the Lord in prayer. God is taking care of His children. You didn't know that, did you? With all the churches, with all the preachers, you would think there wouldn't be a need for this kind of activity on the part of God. What we need to keep in mind is that, *"Many are called, few are chosen"* (Mat. 20:16). Moreover, Jesus said, *"Not every one who says to Me, Lord ,Lord, shall enter the kingdom of heaven..."* (Mat. 7:21). Then again, our elders said the same thing, only in a different way. I'm sure you have heard or even said so yourself, "Everybody talk'n (or sing'n) 'bout heaven ain't going there!"

You may ask, don't we have plenty of Christians, preachers, deacons, trustees, ushers, choir members, missionaries, other church leaders, and church members to help those in need? That's just the point! Yes, we have all of these people and more. But, the question is, "Are they truly committed to Christ?" I am not here to judge your motives, actions, or anything of that nature. That is between you and God. It is none of my business. God alone is the Judge. I am just here doing for God what the marines do for the United States Government, that is, to serve faithfully and submit to authority. It may be said, 'It's not my place to always understand why, but only to do or die.' Somebody's life may depend on my faithfulness to God and my willingness to submit to God's authority. Like the marines, I don't take my job lightly. In fact, the life I save may be my own.

The marines go through a tough selection process looking for a select, few good men and they come up with what they believe to be the best available. They offer a monetary inducement to get a person to join. God is also looking for a few good men, a few good women, a few good boys and girls. If you decide to become a Christian soldier, God offers you so much more than what the marines can offer. Join the ranks today, it doesn't cost you any money to enroll in the army of the Lord. This is so, because Jesus the price for you when He died for your sins on Calvary's cross. This is the case for every one who comes to Christ. God wants to bless you in a special way. His desire is to bless every one, but every one won't let Him. Some people have a certain lifestyle that prevents God from blessing them, and consequently they do not reap the benefits available to them according to the promises of God.

Before I tell you what the benefits are, let me state the requirements are in order for you to receive special blessings from God. You in particular, not anyone else, but **you**, despite the fact that God is no respector of persons. He wants to bless you. Please remember, I have made the announcement that God is looking for a few good people. When you join the army of the Lord there are six areas in your life God is going to focus on to toughen you up for life's battles.

First, you must be willing to listen to God, read the bible, and learn about His word. That is where you get your instruction on how to govern your life in everyday living. That is where you learn about God, who He is, what He did, and what He is doing. This is essential. You must be willing to listen. You'll also learn a lot about yourself: Who you are; Where you came from; and, Why you are here.

Second, you must be faithful and obedient to God, not to me, man or woman, husband or wife, king or nation, mother or father, pastor or priest, etc. If it came to a situation in life there should not be a moment or hesitation regarding your faithfulness and obedience to God.

Third, you must develop patience. God is going to put you in many situations that will give you the patience of Job. With Job-like patience, getting through the harsh realities of life become easier. Getting pass some problems will even seem like a cake walk. These situations may take place at home, at school, at work, at play, or at church. You will miss out on many blessings from God if you don't have patience (Isaiah 40:28-31).

Fourth, you must practice forgiveness, none of this mess about 'I will forgive you, but I won't forget' garbage. That is absolute nonsense, it means absolutely nothing to God. God will work with you in that area, if you let Him.

Fifth, you must be courageous. You cannot be a timid, cowardly, vacillating, wishy-washy, joker, and expect God to bless you. It won't happen. You have to have convictions and be willing to stand for them. Everybody knows what God did with the church at Laodicea. He spewed them out of His mouth (Rev. 3:16).

And *sixth*, you have to love everybody. None of these character traits are developed easily, all of them take time for growth. We are constantly working on them, but the one that seems to be most difficult is the command, not request, to love one another, even our enemies. This for some people is too much. They cannot get over this hurdle, and they wonder why God doesn't bless them. To me, it is all too obvious. But let's read what the word of God has to report on this matter:

Beloved, let us love one another, for love is of God; and everyone who loves is born of God and knows God. He who does not love does not know God, for God is love....If someone says, "I love God," and hates his brother, he is a liar; for he who does not love his brother whom he has seen, how can he love God whom he has not seen? And this commandment we have from Him: that he who loves God must love his brother also.
[1 John 4:7-21]

God's Boot Camp

After you have enlisted in the armed service, you are sent to a special base for orientation, training, and the like. You have no status. You are considered to be a raw recruit. You must be taught many things before you are ready to go out to meet your foe, the enemy. If you do not get the proper training, you will become an accident waiting to happen and many people, including yourself, may be hurt or killed. One reason we have so many problems in our churches is because too many of our people suffer from a lack of proper training. We have the blind leading the blind. We have leaders who say, "Don't do as I do, but, do as I say." We have leaders with no vision. Where there is no vision the people perish (Prov. 29:18). We have leaders who are trying to teach what they don't know and they want to lead you where they will not go. God's boot camp will change all of that.

When you come to God, just as you are, you are a sinner saved by the Grace of God. You still have all of your low-down, dirty, filthy, sinful nature that nobody, but nobody can change but God. No school, no doctor, no seminary, no psychologist, or psychiatrist can change these ways. But thanks be to God, they can be changed, but only by God. When you come out of God's boot camp your hands will be new. Your feet will be new, too. Now these events may not happen all at once. It is going to take some time, but through regeneration and the process of sanctification you will have a new mind, you will think new thoughts, and you will have a new walk. You will sing a new song. God is preparing you for His service. God is still preparing me. Please be patience with me, God is not through with me yet. I'm not what I ought to be, but I'm not what I use to be. God is not through with me yet.

You will notice that in the list of qualifications given to be blessed of God, certain things were not mentioned. Gender was not mentioned (male or female), race was not mentioned (red, yellow, black or white), age was not mentioned (young or old), educational degree was not mentioned, socioeconomic status was not mentioned, where you live was not mentioned, birthplace and national origin was not mentioned, martial status was not mentioned, nor physical stature. God asks only two basic questions of everybody. These are: (1) "Are you willing to be obedient to me and my word, and abide by its teachings?"; (2) The second question is, "Are you willing to commit yourself to serve Me, and Me only?" Putting yourself in position to be blessed is a matter of faithfulness and obedience to God.

You already possess all the requirements that God asks of you. I repeat, you already have them. These are character traits. They need to be cultivated and developed, refined. God is going to make and mold you after His will. You have heard and even seen God, the Master Potter, miraculously and skillfully change, shape and mold people before your very eyes. Haven't you heard or perhaps participated in a discussion that goes something like this:

What in the world is happening to So'n'So? He/she has been acting kind of funny lately. He/she is acting kind of strange, peculiar. His/her wife/husband told me So'n'So just got 'religion'. That 'religion' thing is something else. It makes you do some strange things. Who would have thought that So'n'So would have cleaned up his/her act and decide to straighten up and fly right?

Let us be careful at this point. While we do want to recognize and encourage So'n'So to keep on his/her upward journey, we don't want to give him/her too much credit. You see, So'n'So enlisted in the army of the Lord, and God is helping him/her to work it out. God is making and molding So'n'So after God's will.

The Good Part

We know what the armed forces offer to get you to join. The armed forces assures you that you will not have to worry about food, shelter, or clothing. They supply all of that plus they give you some spending money. When I joined I got $21 (dollars) a month and the GI bill -- I went to college. Basic needs are met plus some chump change. Today, your needs are met, plus tuition money for college. God's offer is better. God says in His Word:

- Never have the righteous been seen forsaken or their seed begging for bread (Psalms 37:25).

- God will supply your ever need through Christ Jesus our Lord (Phil. 4:19).

- Jesus came that we might have life, and have it more abundantly, i.e. full of joy, peace, and filled with purpose (John 10:10).

- No good thing will He withhold from those who walk upright (Psalm 84:11).

- Eyes have not seen, ears have not heard,
nor has entered the hearts of men the things
God has prepared for them that love Him
(1 Cor. 2:9).

- *Then Peter began to say unto Him, "See, we have left all and followed You." So Jesus answered and said, "Assuredly, I say to you, there is no one who has left house or brothers or sisters or father, or mother, or wife, or children or lands, for My sake and the gospel's, who shall not receive an hundredfold now in this time -- houses, and brothers, and sisters, and mothers, and children, and lands, with persecutions -- and in the age to come eternal life. But many who are first will be last, and the last first."* [Mark 10:28-31]

God's Reason

What on earth is God doing? God is looking for a few good people. God is looking for people like you. The reason why God wants you is because He wants to bless you and bring some excitement into your life. God wants to bless you so you can be a blessing to some one else. God wants to bless you so you can reflect His goodness and His mercy throughout His creation to His glory. God wants to use you in His service. Are you going to let Him? We want to live so God can use us anytime and anywhere.

Chapter 8

SOME THINGS GOD JUST "DON'T KNOW!"

Scripture: Genesis 1:1-31; Psalms 139:1-18; 23-24

Songs: 1. *How Great Thou Are*
(Carl Boberg, translated by Stuart Hine)
2. *Come to Jesus* (unknown)

Christians through the ages have always believed that God knows everything. He is omniscient, i.e., He knows everything (Psalms 147:5). He is the creator and sustainer of the universe. God is also omnipotent, i.e., all powerful. In addition, He is also omnipresent, that means He is everywhere. The bible teaches this about God. These are three fundamental characteristics about God Christians throughout history have accepted as axiomatic without question or debate.

Keeping this thought in mind, that God knows everything, it can be deduced that there are some things God does not know. This may sound like double talk, or even a contradiction. It is a paradox. It is not for me or any finite mind to say, or even suggest, what God the creator of the universe does or does not know. We are mortal and finite, God is immortal and infinite. Yet, it does seem reasonable in view of the paradoxical nature of the topic at hand to infer on the one hand, and deduce on the other, that there are some very important things that affect our lives that God does not know.

In a strict, logical sense, perhaps, it is not quite right to use the statement, "Some Things God Just Don't Know" for the things God does know are difficult, to say the least, if not impossible to even imagine. This is especially true as we recognize and consider the relationship between the finite and the infinite. Yet, it does appear proper to use this phrase to point out four vital areas that concern and affect our lives in a very personal way. Therefore, I believe an extended explanation for using the phrase is in order. This line of reasoning, and in view of the scriptures read, call for, even demand some explaining.

It would seem that the following line of reasoning justifies using the phrase, "Some Things God Just Don't Know." It should not be taken literally, least we be presented with the absurdity of a contradictory God, which is foreign to the Gospel. When the phrase, "Some Things God Just Don't Know" is used, I mean to suggest that the alternative options available to God with respect to His plan of salvation for man as expressed in the bible, would go against and even contradict His claim to be holy, righteous, good, truthful, and loving.

This is to say, that as we consider God's nature (holy, righteous, truthful, and loving) the promises He has made to us in the bible, as one considers the person and work of Jesus Christ, one reasons that these factors, singular and combined, constitute a binding and limiting force on the actions of God. These limiting factors are self-imposed but they are no less true and no less binding (Numbers 23:19; Titus 1:2).

By virtue of the attribute of truthfulness, which comprises a fundamental basic part of his nature, God cannot arbitrarily act in such a manner as to undermine or destroy the church, cancel or not honor the promises He has made, or nullify the work of Christ. He can not disclaim or destroy the Bible. To act arbitrarily with respect to any one or all of the above is to play havoc with the created universe and contaminate His moral purity.

Since God is creator and sustainer, He can do anything He wills, but, and this is a big but, since God has promised never again to destroy the earth by flood, and has given the rainbow as a reminder of that promise, He cannot destroy the world by flood at will. Some may rightly say, or ask, can not God change His mind just as anyone else can? The answer is obviously yes, but, not without drastic changes, with grave repercussions, in the character of God, the salvation that God offers, God's promises in the bible, the nature of the church, and in a very real sense, it would mean that God is not who He says He is (in His word). This would mean that God is not trustworthy. This would also be an indication of the fact that whatever action man took in relation to God as outlined in the bible would be subject to be undermined to say the least, if not totally destroyed. Faith in such an inconsistent, changeable, and untrustworthy god would encourage belief in fables, false hopes, and fanciful illusions. God, even God can not afford this. The price is too high. The foundation of the church will have been undermined, if not destroyed and the eternal longing of man to be with his maker will have been dealt a debilitating blow. Remember, we are dealing with an "If...,Then...." situation.

We have already noted in a brief passing manner something about what God can or cannot do. For the remaining time let us consider what an omniscient, all-knowing God "Don't know."

The Church

"Some Things God Just Don't Know." God does not know of a more appropriate means to display His Glory than the gathering of Believers in the church!!

You must be joking! You got to be kidding! All those liars, whoremongers, thieves, hypocrites, and who knows what or who else. You mean to tell me this so-called great and mighty God can't do any better than that?

You must keep in mind that different people have different points of views and perceptions of what they see and experience. Your view of the church may be out of line, completely out of focus with that of God's. You see a building, something great and magnificent. Others, not so great and, perhaps, run down. God may or may not see none of these. You may see scattered over the land, groups of poor, pitiful, struggling, misguided, weak, creatures which band together with like-minded souls. God sees faithful soldiers on the battle field, fighting the good fight of faith. The sanctuary, the building, the physical facility is the gathering place for the 'ekklesia', the called out ones. Those who are in the world but not of the world. Those born again Believers who have, or are putting on the armor of God. Those who walk by faith, not by sight. You may not think much of the church, but it is God's creation, purchased by water and blood. Christ loved it so much He gave His life for it.

This local congregation may or may not be a poor representation of God's glorious creation, and its witness in many instances may come off as timid and unconvincing but that is not the true story. In the local church God meets and greets His Believers with the presence of His precious Holy Spirit. The Holy Spirit who quickens, who enlightens, who gives hope and sustains our faith, who wipes our weary eyes and gives hope to our fainting hearts. It is in God's church that burnt out lives and disappearing hopes are revitalized, aspirations are born and sustained. With this kind of perspective we can understand why David declared, *"I would rather be a doorkeeper in the house of my God than dwell in the tents of wickedness"* (Ps. 84:10).

The local church, the one you see most often, and most familiar with, is only one dimension of a much more significant revelation of God's church. The local church is part of the universal church. The universal church consists of all Believers from every nation, kindred, tribe, of all ages and from all generations. This is also described as being the church triumphant and the bride of Christ. The glorious church! The church triumphant! Many of our local churches have become domesticated, even tame. As a consequence their witness is limited.

It is the universal church that Jesus, the Son of the living God, declares the gates of Hell shall not prevail. It is in local churches around the world that believers congregate, fellowship, worship, and learn about God and His relationship to His people. Here God's Holy Spirit pours out His abundance of blessings and information about how we are to conduct our lives in relationship to God, ourselves, and other humans in a way that honors God and brings glory to God. If God wants us to have such a wonderful relationship with Him and others, and He does because the bible tells us so, then He should, and did, provide the means to carry out the task. Since God has elected primarily, but not exclusively to use the church for this purpose, which brings Him glory, it is reasonable to conclude that God does not know of any better means to get the job done, than to use the church.

The Bible

More things God, "Don't know." God does not know of a better means to get you to know about Him than what is presented in the bible.

Written by inspired men directed by the Holy Spirit the bible is the primary source of information by which we can learn what we need to know about God, the world we live in, the problem of sin and death, and God's plan for human salvation. It is from the pages of scripture that we learn about the character of God, of His creative powers, of His righteouness/justice, of His goodness and mercy, of His love, and of His grace. Where else can we find so much real, valuable, reliable information about God than in the Bible. The truth is, the bible is a store house of knowledge regarding who God is, what He does, and what His motives are. Because of this God does not know of a better way to foster and maintain communications between Himself and His highest creation, man.

No other bountiful source of reliable knowledge can be found nor is there available from no other place, so much real, practical information on how we can, and should relate to God, to ourselves, to our church, our family, our surrounding environment, and our world. Is it any wonder that David declares, *"Your word is a lamp unto my feet and a light unto my path"* (Ps. 119:105) and, *"Your word I have hidden in my heart That I might not sin against You"* (Ps. 119:11).

Note what the apostle Paul stated when he charged young Timothy to preach the word:

> *All Scripture is given by inspiration of God, and is profitable for doctrine, for reproof, for correction, for instruction in righteousness, that the man of God may be complete, thoroughly equipped for every good work. I charge you therefore before God and the Lord Jesus Christ, who will judge the living and the dead at His appearing and His kingdom: Preach the world! Be ready in season and out of season. Convince, rebuke, exhort, with all longsuffering and teaching. For the time will*

> *come when they will not endure sound doctrine, but according to their own desires, because they have itching ears, they will heap up for themselves teachers; and they will turn their ears away from the truth, and be turned aside to fables. But you be watchful in all things, endure afflictions, do the work of an evangelist, fulfill your ministry.* [2 Tim. 3:16-17; 4:1-6]

"Some Things God Just Don't Know." No, God does not know of a better means to get you and I to know more about Him. If He did, we believe He, in all of his wisdom, would do it. After all, *"...no good thing will he withhold from those who walk uprightly"* (Ps. 84:11).

Your Selfworth and the Bible

God wanted you to know just how valuable you are. He wanted you to know how precious and special you are so He did not entrust the enormous, and grave responsibility of placing value on our lives to any one group who may or may not have a vested interested in the outcome of the evaluation. No, God told you Himself through the pages of the bible not only what you are and who you are, but whose you are. This matter is intensely personal, but not entirely private. Thus identification of the individual is no private matter.

> *For God so loved the world that He gave His only begotten Son, that whoever believes in Him should not perish but have everlasting life.* [John 3:16]

Behold what manner of love the Father has bestowed on us, that we should be called children of God.... [1 John 3:1]

God wanted not only for you to know how precious, how valuable, how important you are, but just as significant, He wanted everyone else to know as well. So He put this extremely vital information in His word. He entered it in such a manner so that anyone from grammar school to post graduate scholar can read and understand what it says and mean, believing it is an entirely different matter.

Your value as an individual is preeminent, to say the least, to your race, gender, age, education, social status, political orientation, economical position, or environmental circumstances. As important as they are, these are relative and subordinate to the fact that God created you in His own image and likeness. So what is the big deal? What difference does it make? If any? It makes all the difference in the world.

To see yourself as a son or daughter of God, the creator of the universe, influences, even determines your attitude toward yourself (negative or positive), your family and friends, your environment, your world. Knowledge of God gained from a faithful reading and studying of the Bible aids us in gaining a proper understanding of who God is, His character, His role in the world, and in our lives. This faithful reading and studying of the bible also gives us a proper understanding of who we are, what we are, how we got here, why we are here, who we belong to, and who we have to answer to. God wanted you to know about yourself. Not only did He want you to know about yourself but also about your relationship to Him and the rest of His creation. He had to find a way to make you aware of all of this. Since God has elected to contain this vital information in the sacred scriptures, we can draw no other conclusion, but that God does not know of any better manner to reveal this information to you than through the bible.

That Time Thing

Here is another thing that God "Don't know." God does not know of a better time than now for you to get your life in order. There are many things in our lives, and our environment, that we are aware of but come as a puzzle, a riddle, a paradox, or even a contradiction. There are many intangibles that nag at our ability to understand them. One of these phenomena is what we call time. How do you know it is there, that it is reality? You can't see time. You can't feel or touch it, hear it, taste it or smell it. Yet, we know it to be a reality we cannot avoid. We must come to grips with the reality of time. Look in the mirror and you will see the reality of the 'Then' and 'Now' picture.

We have read and heard it said, *"A thousand years are but a day in the sight of God"* (Ps. 90:4; 2 Pet. 3:8). But, for you and I, we should harbor no such expectations. Three score years and ten is our allocation on this earth (Ps. 90:10), and it is by the grace of God. Many of us go far beyond this. Even so, we spend our lives as a tale that is told (2 Cor. 3:2,3). Since the earth is the Lord's and the fullness thereof (Ps. 24:1), one may inquire, "What are you doing with God's time?" Are you constantly complaining about what happened in the past, about somebody who done you wrong? Do you often think about what might have been or what should have been or what would be the case if only this or that had been otherwise?

There is much complaining of one kind or another in our communities. For example, take unemployment. Does the high unemployment rate indicate a lack of need for work to be done or a lack of employment opportunities? Quite contrary, the harvest is no less ripe today than when

Jesus first pointed it out (Matt. 9:37-38). Despite sociologically sophistication and technological advances, we still live, to a very large degree, in a spiritually bankrupt era in which the dominant motif is basically selfish and materialistically oriented. I got to get mine no matter what the cost or who gets hurt. I get you before you get me. We are afraid and trust no one. Not friend, family, nor foe. Not even God. How will you deal with Proverbs 3:5-6 ?

The truth of the matter is God does not know of a better time for you to take inventory of your life. That is, where you have come from, where you have been, what shape you are in now, and in what direction you are headed. There is no better time than now. What are you doing with your life?

We are bent on acquiring possessions we cannot truly own, or fully control. In this rat race to keep up with the "Jones", our compassion for others takes a back seat. In view of this, not only must we revisit the question, "What are you doing with God's time?" but, we must also ask, "If not now - when? If not here - where? If not you - who?"

A Few More Things God Does not Know

What else, "Don't God Know?" God does not know of a more important person than you. You are of the utmost value to Him. You were made in His image and likeness. You are special. You are unique and so valuable that He sent His Son, Jesus to die on Calvary in order that you might have the hope of eternal life, a right to the tree of life, and the experience of redemption, propitiation, and reconciliation.

God does not know of a more appropriate place than this location for you and I to make a new commitment to God. We must choose to work in the vineyard while it is still day. The harvest is still ripe, the laborers remain few.

Make a commitment today, don't delay. Do it now. If not now, when? Do it here. If not here, where?

"Some things God Just Don't Know." God does not know of a more significant moment than now for you to deal with Pilate's age old question, *"What then shall I do with Jesus who is called Christ"* (Matt. 27:22)? What then shall you do with Jesus who is called Christ? Years ago the crowd said, "Crucify Him." What do you say. He gave you a free will. Their mistake was that they thought that if they killed Him, they would not have to deal with Him anymore. **EVERY KNEE MUST BOW TO CHRIST AND EVERY TONGUE GIVE ACCOUNT OF HIMSELF TO GOD** (Rom.14:11-12 cf. John 5:22-23). Sooner or later, you and I must come face to face with Jesus and give account for how we lived our life. Get to know Jesus now as your personal savior and friend and eliminate the fear you will have when you meet Him later as Judge. Why don't you accept Him in your heart right now. Let Him rule in your Life today. He loves you so much. He has already proven it. Invite Him to work a miracle in your life today.

Come to Jesus,
Come to Jesus,
Come to Jesus just now;
Just now
Come to Jesus,
Come to Jesus just now.

He will save you,
He will save you,
He will save you just now;
Just now
He will save you,
He will save you just now.

He is able.
He is willing.
Come confess Him.
Come, obey Him.
He will hear you.
He'll forgive you.
He will cleanse you.
Jesus loves you.
Only trust Him.
Come to Jesus (unknown author)

Chapter 9

DRESSED FOR DEFENSE

Scripture: Ephesians 6:10-17

Songs: 1. *Am I a Soldier of the Cross?* (Issac Watts)
2. *I am on the Battlefield for My Lord*
(Sylvana Bell & E.V. Banks)

For all practical purposes, the situations surrounding our lives determine how we dress, what clothes we will wear and when we will wear such clothing. We do not wear spring clothes in the winter nor would we go out to play football in a basketball uniform. We dress for specific situations and circumstances. Today, for this occasion, many of us are dressed in our "Sunday clothes" and even some of us have put on our "shouting" shoes. Soldiers at war do not wear football clothing. As a born again, professing Christian, you are considered by God to be a soldier. You are a soldier in the army of the Lord.

Just as men prepare themselves to meet their enemy or foe, God prepares His people for meeting the enemy. God wants you and I to live victorious lives. Therefore, He instructs us and prepares us accordingly. This is what dressed for defense is all about.

-Stay tuned, don't change that channel, or turn that dial -

The Enemy -- Alive and Well

Defense by definition, implies, or suggest the existence of an enemy or foe (real or imagined). If you did not have an enemy, or a foe, what would you defend? The bible is very clear on this matter. Those of us who honestly believe in God most certainly have enemies who are bent on hurting, harming, killing, and destroying us. If we fail to acknowledge this fact, we place ourselves in a vulnerable position which will render our commitment and testimony to Christ as weak and ineffective, to say the least.

One of our best pieces of defense is the knowledge that we have an enemy. The enemy is alive. If you don't admit you have an enemy or a problem, you will never be able to defend against it or solve it. Also, if you do not realize you have an enemy, you will never stand in the victory circle. Realizing that you have an enemy, recognizing that enemy, and knowing as much as possible about that enemy is one of the best lines of defense you can have.

The bible tells us that our enemy is spiritual in nature. Therefore, bombs, bullets, tanks, and military aircraft will not be effective in dealing with this foe. Just as you cannot not kill an idea with a bullet or stab it to death with a knife, the use of conventional physical means to engage in spiritual warfare is ineffective. For a few moments, we are going to be dealing in an effective manner, with the type of equipment we need to defend ourselves and who is the source of our supplies. What happens when we run low, or run out? How dependable is our supplier? Can the supplier be relied upon in the time of need? This is what this messaged ***Dressed for Defense*** is all about.

In order to be victorious in battle, we need to know at least two things. One, we must know, not think, we must know and be certain who it is we are fighting. Winning a battle with the wrong opponent is no victory.

As Christians we know who our enemy is. It is the devil. We are dealing with the many ways he seeks to disrupt and destroy our lives. To win, we must wear a certain kind of uniform. This uniform is described for us in Ephesians 6:10-17.

The Girdle of Truth

"Stand therefore, having girded your waist with truth,..." (Eph. 6:14). Truth is available. Jesus said, *"I am the way, the truth, and the life. No one comes to the Father except through Me"* (John 14:6). This truth is available to everyone. It can and must be learned. If we would be faithful to God, we would learn and accept this truth of God, we would be guided by these truths in our daily lives, and we would proclaim it everywhere we go.

We must be truthful in all of our endeavors and relationships. We must be truthful in our relationship with God and our relationships with each other. In our worship service, some people will go out of their way, clear across to the other side of the sanctuary, just to keep from meeting or saying something to another brother or sister. That is not being truthful to God, or to our fellow brothers and sisters.

We must be truthful in our relationship to the Bible. How can we expect to win a battle, or fight against our foe, if we do not know God's word? We must take Paul's admonition to young Timothy seriously,

> *Be diligent to present yourself approved to God, a worker who does not need to be*

> *ashamed, rightly dividing the word of truth.*[2 Tim. 2:15]

If you or I expect to win the many battles we must fight, we must be truthful.

We have to gird our loins with truth regarding ourselves. Some people are so mixed up in their thinking, they permit others to define who they are and what they ought to be about.

> -That's not you, take that wig off! Please, you're hurting my eyes.
>
> -You look silly with that toupee. That's not you. Go with the natural look.
>
> -Don't hang out with them, you have an image to uphold. That's not you.
>
> -Don't shop there. What would people say if they saw you in that store?

Why do we have to fake it so much to get along in this world? God did not make a mistake when He created you and I. We are unique individuals. We are fearfully and wonderfully made. Here I am, what you see is what you get. No surprises. We need to stop being so phony, hypocritical, deceptive and resolve to put on the girdle of truth.

Make no mistake about it, just because you have on the girdle of truth, do not make the mistake, or be deceived into believing that you will win a lot of friends and be popular. That just won't happen. The truth of the matter is, the truth is dangerous. Yes, the truth is dangerous because it sheds light in dark places. Jesus said men hate the light because their deeds are evil (John 3:19). Nevertheless, not because of, but despite of this possible situation, you are not well equipped to fight the enemy if you do not girdle up your loins with truth. After all, it was Jesus who said, *"And you shall know the truth, and the truth shall make you free"* (John 8:32).

The Breastplate of Righteousness

We all must wear the breastplate of righteousness. Nobody is perfect. We are all sinners saved by the grace of God. The preacher, the deacon, the trustee, the usher, the choir member, and the pew sitter. Yet, God has an expectation of each one of us. God's word teaches that we can do all things through Christ who strengthens us (Phil. 4:13). We are traveling through this barren land on a road that is likened to a mountain railroad. We experience twists and turns, ups and downs, we experience joys and sorrows, and the agony of defeats and the ecstasy of victories. At one time or another, these have been our experiences in life. Yet in the mist of these experiences, God has an expectation of us, i.e., behavior wise. He wants to be proud of us. He wants to stick out His chest and brag about how good His sons and how good His daughters are. He wants to be proud of His children. "He is My son, she is My daughter!"

A mother once said, "I have to own them because I gave birth to them, but the way they act, I am so ashamed, I would get rid of them, but I can't." God feels that same way about some of us whenever our conduct is so unbecoming of a child of God. God wants us to put on the breastplate of righteousness. It is not such a hard thing to ask of children. After all, we are God's children. He created us. He made us. He knows all about us. Why do we have to act so ugly sometimes? What are we trying to prove? We are still the light of the world. Let your light shine so we can glorify our heavenly Father. We are still the salt of the earth. Let us get our acts together. Let us make a diligent effort to do what is right and pleasing unto God, who does all things well. He is too wise to make a mistake, too loving to be unkind.

Let it not be said of us, "I can't hear what you say because I see what you do." Your enemy is watching you just like God. He knows your weak points. He knows your strengths. Suppose you know something that's not right and you want to say something about the matter. Your enemy says to you, "You better not say nothing, keep your mouth shut and keep your thoughts to yourself." In this situation you are not properly dressed. You do not have on the breastplate of righteousness. Suppose you say something but then try to take it back and act as if you don't know nothing. You are not wearing the breastplate of righteousness. Satan will eat you alive and his co-horts will have a field day, in your face and behind your back. However, if you resist the devil, he will flee from you. You just do right and let the Lord fight your battles. I guarantee you victory will be yours.

-Please be patient with me, God is not through with me yet-

Gospel Shoes of Peace

Gospel is a Greek word that means "good news." Everything being equal, there should be excitement and anticipation when we come to church. We are sick and tired of what we've been hearing all week. On our TV's and radios. We hear of one disaster or of some misfortune that has befallen someone else somewhere in our community or around the world. When we come to church we expect something different. We have had our fill, indeed our cup is running over with one disaster after another. We want and need a breather. Therefore, we go to somebody's church, thinking, believing, and hoping to be encouraged, and inspired. That is what the "Gospel of Peace" is all about. Jesus said,

> *Peace I leave with you, My peace I give to you; not as the world gives do I give to you. Let not your heart be troubled, neither let it be afraid.* [John 14:27]

If you go to church, I don't care what church it is, Baptist, Methodist, Catholic, a White or Black congregation or mixed, if you or I, or anyone else, go to worship with that congregation and leave not knowing more than you did before you entered (not talking about gossip), there is a problem in that situation. You should pray to God to intervene and assist in straightening it out. Don't you try to do it alone. You are not smart enough and besides, it is God's church (at least it is supposed to be). He has already worked it out, while you are trying to figure it out.

If we are going to be victorious in our battles, we are going to have to stay in tune with the Gospel of Peace. We should wear our gospel shoes at all times. If you examine the shoes you are wearing, they may or may not look pretty, they may or may not fit well, they may or may not cost much, they may or may not be this or that (Air Jordan's, Nike, Reebok,...); but, if you are wearing the shoes shodden with the Gospel of Peace, then you're wearing the shoes of a champion! Victory shall be yours in Christ Jesus!

The Shield of Faith

The Bible teaches that without faith it is impossible to please God. What is faith? The Bible also teaches that,

"...faith is the substance of things hoped for, the evidence of things not seen" (Heb. 11:1).

Faith in God is the essence of the Christian religion. The scripture teaches that,

> *...without faith it is impossible to please Him, for he who comes to God must believe that He is, and that He is a rewarder of those who diligently seek Him.* [Heb. 11:6]

In this respect, God has promised that if we diligently seek Him, we will find Him (Prov. 8:17). We must believe what God has promised, He will deliver. God is dependable. He is trust worthy.

Wearing the shield of faith will allow us to quench all the fiery darts of the wicked. The Believer will be tempted by the devil, but faith in God will enable him/her to resist all temptations. This is one part of your dress you should never leave at home, or at church, or at your job, or at play. Take your faith in God with you wherever you go. On land, on sea, or in the air. Don't leave home without it. You and I need God, each and every day of our lives. Every hour, every minute, every second, every moment.

Faith in God provides you and I with the ultimate in security, protection, and peace of mind. The "Good Hands" people at Allstate can't compete. The folks down at American Express say you shouldn't leave home without the card. They can't compete. Faith in God is the card you need to take with you wherever you go. He provides the best in security and protection, He's the best, better than all the rest. Try Him today, don't delay. Pick up the shield of faith!

The Helmet of Salvation

The phrase "Helmet of Salvation" refers to deliverance from the guilt, corruption, and the grip of sin which once ruled over our lives. In fighting this kind of battle, we do not need the excess, weighty baggage of our former lives. When we are confronted by others in this area, we can always say, "I am free, I have been washed in the blood of the lamb." Also, "My sins are forgiven and He has washed me as white as snow." You may also repeat the known fact that, "God is not through with me yet, He is still working with me." However, you may also note, "I may not be what I ought to be, I may not be what I am going to be, but thanks be to God, I am not what I used to be!"

The Sword of the Spirit

Of all the items we have indicated as necessary to be properly dressed to defend the faith, none is more significant than the "Sword of the Spirit." The word of God is the most powerful and potent weapon one can have in his/her defense against any enemy or foe. David has declared, *"Your word I have hidden in my heart, That I might not sin against You"* (Ps. 119:11). He also wrote, *"Your word is a lamp to my feet And a light to my path"* (Ps 119:105). The admonition to young Timothy was to,

> *Be diligent to present yourself approved to God, a worker who does not need to be ashamed, rightly dividing the word of truth.*
> [2 Tim. 2:15]

When Jesus was tempted by the devil, Jesus used the word to defeat him.

Nothing can defeat the devil like the word of God. Through it we know who God is, what He is like, what He did, what He is doing, and what He is going to do. From the word of God we learn about ourselves, where we came from, where we are going, and what will happen to us when we reach our destination. That, brothers and sisters, is a lot of very valuable information. If we spent more time studying the word, we would learn more about God and we would have more confidence in ourselves. The proper use of God's word assures victory. God's word is essential if we are to fight the good fight of faith.

Praying Always

God's word says that we should, *"Pray without ceasing"* (1 Thess. 5:17). It also states that we should:

> *Be anxious for nothing, but in everything, by prayer and supplication, with thanksgiving, let your request be made known to God.* [Phil, 4:6]

Prayer is the key to the kingdom, faith unlocks to door. Prayer is the means by which we get power and communicate with God. To get in touch with headquarters, we must pray. We get our instructions from headquarters.
From headquarters we plan our strategy. When we need help, we call headquarters. The lines of communication are always open. Jesus is on the main line. Call Him up, call Him up, tell Him what you want. You can go and I can go to God in Prayer. If you have not been in touch with God at headquarters, now is the time. If we ever needed the Lord before, we sure do need Him now. Call Him up, call Him up.

Are you dressed properly for defense?

Chapter 10

THREE DIMENSIONS OF LIFE

Scripture: Philippians 3:1-15

Songs: 1. *Higher Ground* (Johnson Oatman, Jr.)
2. *Amazing Grace* (John Newton)

Whatever our conception of man is, most people have come to know him as a three-dimensional individual. We think of ourselves as individuals who are composed of a body (our total physical make-up); a soul (that portion of us that includes our mind, emotions, and will); and spirit (spiritual conscientiousness). We cannot give a precise definite, definition of the soul and spirit as they are used somewhat interchangeably in scripture; but, we do know for sure that they represent a vital and integral part of our nonphysical existence. It cannot be denied. We may, and do have many different ideas and opinions regarding the make-up and role of each one of these aspects of our lives. After all, great philosophical debates have grown out of the awareness of these differences. Some believe that humans are merely two dimensional beings composed of physical and nonphysical components. Yet, I believe it is safe to say, that it is helpful to think of humans as being three-dimensional.

Not only are we three-dimensional in our physical make up, we are three-dimensional in our orientation towards life. Our actions rise out of the three-dimensional prone upon which all human existence rests: the past;

present; and, future. We act and interact with each other with all of these dimensions in mind. For example, two young people are courting one another in the present. This relationship has developed because of what has happened in the past and both of them are looking toward the future. She has definite hopes and plans of escorting that brother to the altar. He's interested in escorting her to the bedroom. Well....

Psychologist, and others in position of knowledge, tell us that overemphasizing, or over-indulgence in any one of these areas in our lives can lead to an imbalance in our mental and psychological make up. A person can dwell and linger so much on the past to such that he or she cannot participate in the present in a meaningful way. And, of course, in a situation like that, the future is lost. The long, nostalgic look into the past, reliving the "good old days" of by-gone years has been the graveyard for countless promising ventures. Orientation, or concentration upon the future, in the form of day-dreaming, or wishful thinking, can and often does, cause many of us to lose sight of the present realities of the day. Not only is the future lost, but all could be lost. Living each day with no regard for the past or present is also problematic.

Here again, illustrations of this nature, indicate the three-dimensional character of human existence. There are other ways the three-dimensional character of man may be indicated. I would like to focus primarily on the three-dimensional aspect of man that relates to height, depth, and width.

Height

Height has several references in the English language. Height in relation to one's personal appearance or stature: too short, too tall, etc.... Height refers to the topmost point of anything: height of a tree, building, tower, etc... That height refers to the highest limit. The greatest degree. The extreme. The climax. The culmination point. For example, it is the height of absurdity that he should propose such a ridiculous idea or scheme. Height also refers to a relatively great distance from top to bottom, or the relatively great distance above a given level. Finally, height refers to a point or place considerably above most others, eminence, elevation. It is to all of these meanings and most especially the latter, that my reference to height is directed.

With any reference to height, a norm, a standard is given or assumed, otherwise references to height become meaningless. Indications of height, as given above, are to be considered in relation to the following questions. How tall do we stand in relationship to the issues and concerns of our society today (drugs, alcoholism, teenage pregnancy, abortion)? How tall do we stand in relation to the issues, needs, and concerns of this church? Only you and God know the true answer to that, so don't try to answer that question just to be saying something. However, just for the record, one can get a pretty accurate indication of how high you and I stand in relation to these and other matters is by the attitude we bring to the situation. You see brothers and sisters, it is our attitude that determines what we will do, if anything at all. It is our attitude that determines when we will do it, if anything at all. It is our attitude that determines where we will do it, if we do it at all. In other words, it is your attitude that will determine what, if any, action you will or will not take. Your attitude will dictate how high you will go in relation to this and any other activity in life you so choose to be identified with.

Depth

Let us consider depth. Here we go again to the dictionary for help in understanding what this word means. In the dictionary I used, there were five different meanings. I shall consider only two: (1) Deepness, distance below the surface, or from the observer in any direction; (2) That which is deep, as the ocean depths.

Hear this paradox. The tallest, the highest, the strongest building, or sturdiest home can never come into existence until a hole has been dug first. When the deep hole has reached a solid foundation upon which the footing can be placed and then, and only then, one can begin to build the foundation. If this does not happen, the building will never rise very high nor will it be strong.

This is so true in our lives. If we would be strong in the Lord and the power of His might, then we must dig deep into God's word. We are going to have to take seriously Paul's admonition to young Timothy:

> *Be diligent to present yourself approved to God, a worker who does not need to be ashamed, rightly dividing the word of truth.* [2 Tim. 2:15]

How deep are we in the word of God? How deep do we want to be? Have we dug down into the depth of God's word? Are we rooted and grounded in the eternal word of the living God? Do we want the Lord to lift us up and plant our feet on solid ground? We want to dig deep and declare on Christ the solid rock we stand, all other ground is sinking sand.

Width

Here is another paradox. If a man or woman cannot rise tall unless he or she digs deep, that same person cannot dig deep unless he or she first spreads out. For example, sometimes after going to a general doctor, we are referred to a specialist, a person who has spent a very long time and spent a lot of money to gain that position in life. But, only after getting a variety of general courses in medicine, can he or she concentrate the remaining portion of studies in the area of selected specialty. He or she is not just a doctor but a doctor who has specialized in a certain area of medicine. An understanding of the whole body is a prerequisite for specialization in medicine. An understanding of the whole body is neccessary in order to understand how the area of specialty interrelates with the whole body. So it is with some of us. If we are going to grow, we must spread our horizons. Our vision is too narrow and our thinking too narrowminded. People who are deep are visionary and their thoughts are broadminded. There is an openness about them. They are confident. They are not easily intimidated by any given situation.

How much width do we have when it comes to your church? How much width do we have when it comes down to being compassionate with one another? How much width do we have when it comes down to being patient and considerate of one another?

Height, Depth, and Width in Relation to God

Let us now consider height, depth, and width in relationship to God, who is the norm, the standard by which all of our conduct is measured.

Height

God's love is so high you can't get over it! Usually when we think of love, we think in sentimental terms. We usually reserve the use of that word and direct it to someone of special interest to us, a mother, a father, son or daughter, a husband or wife, a sweetheart, boyfriend or girlfriend. In some situations, our use of the word 'love' may even include a limited circle of friends and acquaintances. In many of these relationships, our expressions of love is hap-hazard and sporadic. We are so 'sometimey'. You know what I mean, if you caught us in a good mood, well, and good. But, if you happen to come upon us when we are not, only God knows what will be the outcome of that experience. We say we have to be especially careful of what we say and/or do in the presence of this or that person, this or that group. We don't want to say or do anything to set off the short fuse. Any talk of love in this context may fall on deaf ears. Because we are so moody and temperamental, we can not think, with any degree of certainty, about how high our love for anyone could be, not even for ourselves. Self-hatred and poor self-image is one big problem for many people today.

God's expression of love is just the opposite. It is at its peak, each and every day, twenty-four-hours, without fail. God, who is omniscient, omnipotent, omnipresent, and immutable, who is the same yesterday, the same today, and the same tomorrow and evermore, constantly pours out His love upon us. The bible teaches that even while we were yet sinners Christ died that you and I might have a right to the tree of life.

When the writer John realized how great and how deep the love of God was towards him and others, he declared, *"What manner of love the Father has bestowed on us, that we should be called children of God"* (1 John 3:1)! That is high. It is the extreme expression of affection, that has little, or nothing to do with sex or the absence of it. This love of God is given without price or cost to you and I (Isaiah 55:1-6). Measured by this standard, how high are we in our relationship to God? To one another? Where does He fit into the scheme of our lives? How high is your love in relationship to your church?

God's Grace

God's grace is so wide you can't get around it! God's grace is so wide, it is simply amazing. There is simply no words to describe it. It is, as the song affirms, amazing! There are no words to describe this act. What is grace? Grace is unmerited favor. It is like someone doing you a favor, when you don't deserve it. Grace is that time when you and I owed somebody money. We were late in paying our bill. We owed the money and we knew it. The payment was due, in fact it was past due. Have you ever been in a situation like that? I have. Many times. My wife and I have been in that type of situation. When it came time to pay the bills, our money being short, we had to decide who was going to be the lucky ones to get some money. Those who did not get any money could have made claims upon us. For whatever reason, they did not. That is grace. They did get paid.

God, the omnipotent one, the omniscient, ever-present, loving father, is like that, even greater. Listen to what Paul says about God's grace as it relates to you and I. In the second chapter of the book of Ephesians, verses nine and ten, He wrote,

> *For by grace you have been saved through faith, and that not of yourselves; it is the gift*

> *of God, not of works, lest anyone should boast.* [Eph. 2:9-10]

That is not only wide, but very wide. There is but one way to describe God's grace, it is simply amazing.

How does your expression of grace towards one another stack up against God's grace? After all, He is the one who set the standard. Does your love of God allow you to be compassionate enough for you to want to be as wide as God is in His grace towards us?

> Amazing grace how sweet the sound,
> that saved a wretch like me!
> I once was lost but now am found,
> Was blind but now I see.
>
> Thro' many dangers, toils and snares,
> I have already come;
> 'Tis grace hath brought me safe thus far,
> And grace will lead me home.
> *Amazing Grace* (John Newton)

We want to pattern our lives after the Lord Jesus Christ, like Paul, we want to press toward the mark, to meet the high calling of God, in Christ Jesus. We want our grace to be wide, wide, so wide that it encompasses the multitudes, not a select few, and reflects the love of our gracious, heavenly Father.

God's Mercy

God's mercy is so enduring and deep, you can't get under it! God's mercy endures forever. That is a very long time. It is also very, very deep. That is why you cannot get under it. No matter how far down you think you are, God's mercy is ever present, even going below that to lift and strengthen and to give new life with a new sense of direction, and purpose. You and I cannot get so low that God cannot reach down, pick us up, turn us around, place our feet on solid ground, put pep in our step, a song in our heart, and get us started on our way in the right direction.

This is what the invitation represents today:

God whose Love is so high,
you can't get over it;
God whose Grace is so wide,
you can't get around it
God whose Mercy is so enduring,
you can't get under it.

God invites you into close fellowship with Him. He wants all of you. Your mind, body, and soul. All three dimensions of your life.

Chapter 11

GREAT DISCOVERIES OF LIFE

Scripture: Genesis 3:7 (1-21)

Songs 1. *Yield not to Temptation* (Horatio R. Palmer)
2. *Trust and Obey* (John H. Sammis)

The word 'discover' is a verb and may be defined in a couple of ways such as: (1) to find out or learn for the first time; (2) to catch sight of; (3) to reveal or make known. No matter what definition one chooses to use, especially "to catch sight of, or to reveal," great discoveries are characterized by apprehension of the unexpected, an element of potential surprise, anxiety, and some fear of the new and unknown. These potentially negative aspects in a person's life are put in check by an attitude of courage, curiosity, and conviction displayed in facing the situation.

> It is dangerous -- we don't know anything about that -- we shouldn't try that.
>
> So what -- let's try it anyway -- let's do it -- let's go for it!

In many ways, these "discoveries" are not dramatic. These are not earth-shaking events. There is no fanfare nor are the discoveries necessarily crowd pleasing. Many times these "discoveries" are not spectacular. Why then, are they called great? They are "great" because of the impact and influence they have on our lives and those with whom we come in contact with. How many times in our lives have you and I said or thought, "Why didn't I think of that before?" or, "If I only knew then what I know now, things would be different." These are "discovery" moments.

Today, our focus of attention on discovery is not confined to the physical dimensions of reality, but to the intellectual, spiritual, emotional, psychological, and ideological as well. The discoveries we are now concerned with embody elements of all these aspects and have a definite impact upon our lives.

Great Discoveries of Life

We will focus on the discovery Adam and Eve made in their relationship to God. There may be some similarities in our lives! The thing that got Adam and Eve in trouble with God was they allowed the serpent the opportunity to sow the seed of doubt, which was fed by the fire of curiosity. It was on these facets of human behavior that put them into a situation to be seduced by the serpent into believing: (1) they would be like God, on the one hand; and (2) that they would not be punished if they disobeyed the command of God. The bottom line of the whole matter boiled down to disbelief in God and the command He had given. In essence, Adam and Eve said, "We don't believe what you say is true." How else could they have committed the act they did?

One can not ignore or discount or even play down the inducing, temptation presented to Adam and Eve by the Serpent, *"...you will be like God, knowing good and evil"* (Gen. 3:5). That's no small fruit! Who among us could resist such a temptation? Nevertheless, Adam and Eve did not get into trouble with God because they were tempted, they got into trouble because they yielded, they gave in. They were tempted with a big fruit, to be sure.

Adam and Eve's basic problem was compounded because of the source of their information. They were deceived, misled by the seductive, inducement (temptation if you will) of one whose reputation and motive they did not check out. Consequently, Adam and Eve acted upon deceptive, misleading, information. Moreover, this information was from a source they failed to investigate. And, more importantly, they should have discussed the matter with God! After all, they were on speaking terms. Even more significant, they did not know of or question the motive of this contemplated action. Why are you telling us this? This question was not asked. Consequently, their discovery amounted to not only a wide, but rude awakening!

They discovered that the price or penalty for disobedience, no matter how unintentional, was not confined to their immediate, temporary discomfort, but to eventual death. *"The soul who sins shall die..."* (Ezek. 18:20). Curiosity does and did, in this instance, kill the cat.

Here, in this situation, we have the first example of passing the buck, or placing the blame on someone else. You know what I mean. I'm talking about refusing to accept responsibility. Here is a situation where an attempt is being made to indicate that the guilty one is not responsible for his/her actions nor the mess he/she has created and/or is in. So Adam's reply to God went something like this,

> All right. God, you asked, "Who told me to do this?" The answer is simple. That woman. The one over there. She is the one who told me it was OK to eat the fruit. She gave it to me. It's not my fault. Don't blame me. She's the one.

Have you ever noticed how bold we get when we try to get the blame off of us and pin it on somebody else? "No, no, no. I didn't do it, she did it!" Bold.

Thus, with Adam, the vicious cycle of blame, fault-finding, and excuses was set into motion:

- Adam blamed Eve
- Eve blamed the serpent
- The husband blames the wife
- The wife blames the husband
- Parents blame the children
- Children blame the neighbors
- The family blames the schools
- The schools blame the families
- The teachers blame the School board
- The School board blames the city
- The city blames the state
- The state blames the government
- The government blames the politicians
- The politicians blame the corporations
- The corporations blame the lawyers
- The lawyers blame the environmentalist
- The environmentalist blame the consumer
- The consumers blame the church
- Church members blame church leaders
- Church leaders blame the devil

How many times have you heard someone say:

- The devil made me do it.

Or even worse:

- God, why did You let this happen!

Nobody, I mean Nobody is ever at fault. We all have good excuses. It is always somebody else's fault. If need be, even the invisible man is blamed! You now how it is. If you have a house full of children and you find an empty milk container in the refrigerator, ask who put the empty container back into the refrigerator and you'll see what I mean when I say the invisible man is even blamed at times.

This reminds me of a story:

> This is a story about four people named *Everybody*, *Somebody*, *Anybody*, and *Nobody*. There was an important job to be done and *Everybody* was asked to do it. *Everybody* was sure *Somebody* would do it. *Anybody* could have done it, but *Nobody* did it. *Somebody* got angry about that because it was *Everybody's* job. *Everybody* thought *Anybody* could do it but *Nobody* realized that *Everybody* wouldn't do it. It ended up that *Everybody* blamed *Somebody* when *Nobody* did what *Anybody* could have done.
> [Source unknown]

You may recall the Lord asked the question, "Who...?" One cannot place too much emphasis upon the, "Who." It represents inquiry. For example, "Who told you this?" "What exactly did he/she/they say?" "Where did this take place?" "When did this take place?" "How did this come about?" Not asking these questions can make a big difference! Make no mistake about it, and do not let anyone deceive you. The gathering and dispensing of information is the biggest game in town. Much effort and much scheming is being employed these days to deceive, mislead, confuse, and misuse folk by providing bits and pieces of false information. Insinuation, innuendo, and manipulation are standard tools of the trade used by prisoners of darkness to camouflage hidden agendas.

The drug pusher doesn't tell you that the product is harmful to your body and health. They say the opposite, that it's good! The tobacco industry doesn't voluntarily tell that their product is harmful to your body and health, they lead you to believe that smoking is a good thing, a cool thing. Satan doesn't tell you that when you seek satisfaction and fulfillment in life apart from God, that what he offers is only illusionary and temporary and that you will ultimately become totally frustrated, unsatisfied, and actually lose your life. He tells that you will not only find satisfaction and fulfillment, but that you will be like God Himself, self-sufficient in all things.

Satan deceived Adam and Eve by providing them with mis-information. They were not told the whole story. They fell for his trick and they had to suffer the consequences. The price was high. They fell out of favor with God and was banished from the garden. Why? Simply because they relied upon not only a half truth, but, upon an out right lie. What was the lie? That they would become as gods on the one hand and that they would not be punished. Many will discover that they do have to give an account of their lives and that they must deal with the consequences.

Who told you that a Holy and Righteous God would not hold you accountable for your every word and deed? Who told you? Who told you that you were the most good-looking, the most handsome, the most gallant, the most beautiful, the most brilliant, and the wisest of all? In other words, who told you that you were the fairest of them all? What mirror are you looking in? What a rude awakening when you look into the mirror of God's word and see you for who you really are. Who told you that the second time around is better than the first? Who told you that the grass is greener on the other side of the fence? Who told you that the darker the berry the sweeter the juice? Who told you that? Who told you that if loving you is wrong, I don't want to be right? Who told you that all that church stuff is not necessary to get into heaven? Who told you that you don't have to be accountable to God for cheating on your taxes? Who told you that there is no Hell? Who told you? Who told you? Who told you that you were a loser? Who told you that you could accomplish nothing? Who told you that you to wait until your old to get right with God? Who told you that you would see the light of a new day? Consider the source. Your life may depend on it. Consider the source.

Wow! What a discovery. What a discovery when you find out that what you heard and what you were told is not the truth. What a rude awakening. God's word tells us, *"Do not be deceived, God is not mocked; for whatever a man sows, that he will also reap"* (Gal. 6:7). My bible also says,

> *For we must all appear before the judgment seat of Christ, that each one may receive the things done in the body, according to what he has done, whether good or bad.*
> [2 Cor. 5:10]

You may discover that you don't have as much time as you think.

Disobedience: The Crux of the Matter

Let us not be deceived, misled, or be side-tracked from the real issue involved in this situation. The fundamental issue here in "Great Discoveries of Life" is one of disobedience, plain and simple. Adam and Eve disobeyed God's command. Disobedience carries with it an automatic penalty of one kind or another.

The penalty disobedience be immediate or delayed. Those in authority to render judgment may decide not to administer the penalty promptly. We often try to get away with as much as we possibly can, but our faults will eventually catch up with us. When that happens, we know we're in trouble, that we're going to get it. As a child, its a terrible feeling to know you're going to get a spanking (whoop'n) for disobeying your parents. When the disobedient person realizes that they have been caught, they may pray to high heaven and wish that he or she were dead. The consequences of disobedience may or may not be slow in coming, but you can be sure of one thing, as the bible states, *"...be sure your sin will find you out"* (Num. 32:23).

Think now about the consequences you suffered for disobeying the advice of mom and/or dad when they told you to stay away from this or that person, group of persons, or situation. Granted, mothers and fathers are not always right, do you remember what you said or thought? Did it go something like this, "My Gosh! Good Grief! Who do they think they are talking to? Don't they realize I can take care of myself? I can't wait until I get out of this house!" Then the day comes, as we all knew would, you leave. After awhile, you may then say or think, "If I knew it was going to be like this I would have stayed home. This is rough!" Now that, my brothers and sisters, is a great discovery.

What about people who smoke cancer sticks, oops, I meant cigarettes. In spite of the warnings, people still don't pay attention. They say to themselves, I know people who have been smoking for years and nothing has happened to them. Then when they turn up with cancer, then they wonder why it happened to them. That's a discovery, but its not too late to quit smoking. In any case, you must deal with the consequences. Just another round in the game of misleading deception.

Marijuana is good for you. I heard doctors prescribe it for glaucoma. Here, try some of this good stuff, see, nothing happened to me. Try this, it'll make you feel good. Before you know it, you aren't afraid of trying some of this and some of that. Depending on the situation, it may be amphetamines, barbiturates, or even crack or cocaine. One day you'll wake up and discover that you're hooked, that you can't go without something to pick you up or calm you down. It may be alcohol or prescribed nerve pills. The discovery comes too late to escape the consequences. You may have been deceived or mislead into believing something to be other than what it really was. But, that is one thing that can happen when one is disobedient. Listen to your conscience, to thine own self be true. The consequences are certain.

How about those students who go to school thinking it to be some kind of a game or joke? They refuse to listen to their parents and teachers. When and if they graduate, they enter the real world and find out that they cannot complete a job application correctly. What a discovery! What a rude awakening for that person who went in for a job opportunity, so confidently and cocky, only to leave feeling so embarrassed and dejected. Can you imagine how that person must have felt?

Everybody talking and singing about heaven 'ain't' going there. The bible says, *"...Behold, to obey is better than sacrifice..."* (1 Sam. 15:22).

One of the characteristics of disobedience is that it produces fear and anxiety. Adam and Eve disobeyed God. Consequently, they got nervous, afraid, they probably also bickered, tried to rationalize the situation, blamed each other, panicked, ran, and finally tired to hide from God.

Disobedience is a by-product of disrespect. They disobeyed because they lost respect for God. They felt no obligation to obey His command. Here is a principle. If you respect a person, you will have no problem with obeying their authority. It is as simple as that. Respect and obedience go together. They go hand-in-hand. Do not try to separate them.

In our Christian journey we have discovered:

- Every good-bye isn't gone.

- All sickness is not until death.

- That terror may reign in the night but joy comes in the morning.

- If we hold our peace, and let the Lord fight our battles, we know that victory shall be ours.

- The Lord will make a way out of no way.

- His yoke is easy and His burden is light.

- There is a way that seems right to a man but in the end is destruction.

- There is no hiding place, no fig tree leaf big enough to hide you or me from the eyes of God.

Like Adam and Eve, many pastors, preachers, deacons, Sunday school teachers, and other so-called Christians are in for a rude awakening when they discover what we all know, "Everybody talking and singing about heaven ain't going there!"

Wow! what a "Great Discovery" it will be when it's all over and Rev. 'High-minded' and deacon 'do good' (you know them, they are all over the place) find themselves in the other place. A whole bunch of ushers and goo-goobs of choir members (I don't know who they are, but God does) are in for a rude awakening when they "Discover" what we all know, "Everybody talking and singing about heaven ain't going there!" Now that's going to be a super big and unfortunate "Great Discovery" for a bunch of church-going, bible-toting, folks!

However, if we run this race with patience, looking to Jesus, the author and finisher of our faith, we will discover, for sure, that we have an eternal dwelling place in the heaven. A place that's not made with hands but whose builder and foundation is God. It's reserved with your name on it. If you think you have seen, heard, thought, or dreamed of the many beautiful and wonderful things available here on this earth, try imagining what it must be like when the bible declares,

> *But as it is written: "Eye has not seen, nor ear heard Nor have entered into the heart of man The things which God has prepared for those who love Him."* [1 Cor. 2:9]

In the mean time let us not get impatient, or weary in well doing. Let us be mindful of the prophet Isaiah when he wrote:

> *Have you not known? Have you not heard? The everlasting God, the Lord, The Creator of the ends of the earth, Neither faints nor is weary. There is no searching of His*

> *understanding. He gives power to the weak, And to those who have no might He increases strength. Even the youths shall faint and be weary, And the young men shall utterly fall, But those who wait on the Lord Shall renew their strength; They shall mount up with wings like eagles, They shall run and not be weary, They shall walk and not faint.* [Isa. 40:28-31]

You don't have to hide from or fear God! This may be your greatest discovery yet. You don't have to hide from or fear God if you are His child. Ask Jesus in your life and enjoy a loving relationship with your heavenly Father. As your Father, He will love you no matter what mistake(s) you have and will make. And because He loves you unconditionally, when you do mess up, He still loves you and accepts you for who you are, His child. You may still have to deal with some consequences, but not from a condemning judge, but, rather from a loving, merciful Father.

Chapter 12

FAITH, FIGHTS, AND CROWNS

Scripture: Eph. 6:10-18; 1 Tim. 6:11-14

Songs: 1. *Am I a Soldier of the Cross?* (Isaac Watts)

Many people have different ideas, or conceptions, of what Christianity is or what it means to be a Christian. Many times, too many of us, who call ourselves Christians, act as though we do not have the faintest idea of what that really means as it relates to our daily lives.

Someone who really understood what it meant, was the Apostle Paul, the writer of the scripture for today. He was aware of what good things that lay ahead for those who believed in God and take His word seriously. But, he was equally, if not more keenly aware of the actions and reactions of men and women as they interacted with each other. A master psychologist, he knew human nature, its potential for good, or for ill. That is why he felt the need to charge Timothy as he did. Paul did not want this young preacher to be under no illusions about the nature of the gospel that he was to preach, nor what impact and influence it would have upon those who heard it.

Paul indicated to young Timothy what a vital faith in Christ can and ought to do for a person who truly believes. Paul did not have any doubts about Timothy's personal commitment, but the people Timothy would come into contact with was a totally different matter. Paul envisioned a time when believers in God will become spiritually weak, disillusioned about God, the church, and about Christ. They will begin to wonder whether they should continue to profess faith in God or get off this pilgrim journey and take another route. Some will even forget who they are, and what they have as a result of their belief in Christ. Paul envisioned that some will cease to think of themselves as disciples of Christ, soldiers of the cross, and followers of the Lamb. They will no longer consider themselves to be defenders of the faith. Paul envisioned that many will become satisfied playing games with their religion, the religiosity game in which they will go to church just out of habit, tradition, or curiosity. With this frame of mind some people bring little or no expectations of what they hope to receive from God, or what they themselves intend to give in the worship experience. In every category, they contribute as little as possible. The power and presence of God's Holy Spirit is not eagerly sought after, or earnestly desired. They come to church with a spirit of emptiness. They bring nothing to church, make no positive contribution, and they will leave with the same spirit of emptiness, feeling and wondering whether or not the whole thing was worth it or just a waste of time. It does not have to be, or stay that way. The time Paul envisioned is upon us.

Be made aware that all who live spiritually anemic lives are not equipped to deal effectively and thoroughly with the vital issues of this day. In this respect, Paul's charge to young Timothy is as relevant now as it was then. The charge declared: (1) How faith in God will enable the believer to be strong; and, (2) That faith in the Lord Jesus Christ not only makes us Christians by definition, but soldiers, fighters, wrestlers (Eph. 6:10-18) in the army of the Lord. With that in mind, the question arises, "Why do we fight? Who are our enemies? What are the means by which we fight or conduct this battle?"

First, and most importantly, we fight because we have an enemy who comes to kill, steal, and destroy us (John 10:10). Secondly, our enemy is none other than the devil and a host of fallen angels (1 Pet 5:8; Rev. 12:9). Thirdly, the means by which we fight is spiritual, it's a spiritual warfare (Eph. 6:10-18). How does this spiritual warfare manifest itself in our daily lives? A fundamental manifestation of the spiritual warfare that we engage in is found in our various attitudes. Remember, for the most part, your actions are determined by your attitudes. Even though actions and various behaviors are also manifestations of our participation in spiritual warfare, actions and various behaviors are merely secondary to the mental aspect of the spiritual battle. In fact, the battlefield of our spiritual warfare is in the mind. What then are some of these attitudes that we must fight?

We Fight the Downward Push of Self

We fight against the negative attitude some people have about themselves. Low self esteem and feelings of inadequacy. Many of us fail to realize who we are in Christ Jesus and what we have as a result of that relationship. We minimize our potential in the area of our new identity in Christ. If we fully understood what that meant, we would hold our heads up high and walk tall. We would stop making excuses for being indifferent, unconcerned, and change our lazy ways of serving God, and rise above the level of mediocrity. We would not be deterred by the weather. Instead of complaining that its too hot, too cold, it's raining, 'ain't' nobody going to be there, we would say, no matter what, this is the day that the Lord has made, let us be glad and rejoice in it. This is an attitude we wrestle against and must fight to bring about a change. In every conceivable situation, the fact remains, this is God's world.

He is still in control of it. We must fight against this attitude of low self-esteem and inadequacy that we all experience.

We do not give ourselves credit for the skills and abilities we have. The low self-esteem and inadequacy syndrome is debilitating. It traps us into thinking, "I can't do this, I can't do that, we can't do this, we can't do that, we don't have this, we don't have that." How silly and stupid this sounds in the light of God's word which teaches us that we can do all things through Christ that strengthens us (Phil. 4:13). We need to be more positive about ourselves in what we and others can do by the power of the Holy Spirit if we put our faith and confidence in the Lord Jesus Christ. God has given all of us at least one spiritual gift. Also, God has created and designed us as unique individuals with a wide variety of talents, skills, and abilities. God desires that we use all that He has equipped us with to glorify Him.

Must Fight Against the Downward Push of Others

We must fight against the downward push of not only self but others as well. Someone is always trying to put you down, or at least, "in your place," whatever that is. You are too fat, too skinny, too tall, too short, too big, too little, too attractive, too ugly, etc. You didn't go to the right school, the right church, you didn't get the right training. You didn't know the right teachers, you didn't get the right grades. You didn't dress appropriately. You may have spent two hours in front of a mirror trying to make yourself look presentable and now that you are finished, you may think you're pretty hot stuff, right? Well, there are some who don't think so. If they had the guts to tell you what they thought to your face, they would tell you that you have on the wrong hat, wrong shoes, wrong coat, wrong colors, etc. According to them, you are a sight for sore eyes.

The downward push continues on. You are not one of us and don't even think about becoming one of us. You live on the wrong side of town. You live in the wrong neighborhood. You are not good enough to play on my team. We don't want you to be on our side. You can't do that, your a woman. You are too young? Oh, there is one other thing I want to mention. You are not the right color. Say what you will, the fact is that many of us still have very color-value consciousness, a lingering hang up in America. You know how that saying goes,

If you are Black, get back;
If you are Brown, stick around;
If you are Yellow, you're mellow;
If you're White, you're right.

That saying is a bunch of mess. So, we must fight against this attitude to reduce its negative impact upon our lives and the lives of others.

The great downward push, the put downs continue. Get out of my face you old woman, you old fool. Leave me alone you feeble-minded old man. Your day is done gone. Don't you know what's happening. It's time for some new blood. It's time for someone young to take over.

You watch your mouth you young whippersnapper. You are still wet behind the ears. You can't tell me nothing. Wait until you are grown, then you might be able to get a word in. Older people who think that some how age has automatically made them wiser have a problem. After all, there is some truth to the statement, there is no fool like an old fool. Young people have hang ups as well. They know everything, after all, this is a new day, a new generation.

They know more than anybody else know so they tell you to butt out and get out of their way.

This mutual disrespect by both, the now and the then generation, is an attitude problem. It is one that will not go away and it must be dealt with in a serious, determined, manner. We must keep in mind that we have to live with one another and that it serves no useful purpose to be antagonistic toward the other. We need each other and the sooner we realize it, the better off we will be.

There is plenty of room, lots of space for both generations in God's kingdom. There is much for both groups to do. We have no need to waste each other's time and energy on petty things. There is a battle to fight and victories to win. Should not we ask ourselves, what, if anything, does this kind of foolish nonsense have to do with our good fight of faith? I submit to you it has nothing to do with it and we ought to cut out such childish things. We should be about doing our Master's will while it is day, for the night comes when no man can work. Thank God there are limits to which people with these kind of attitudes can prevail.

As you can well imagine, people who exhibits theses types of attitudes are not going to roll over and play dead. That won't happen, but, by the grace and power of God, these negative attitudes can be changed.

Attitude of Luke-Warm Christianity

We must take up the challenge and fight the good fight of faith as God gives us grace and courage. We must fight against the spectator luke-warm Christians who come to church just to see what is going on or to be seen. They may say,

> Perhaps, if the minister is not too long-winded and if he doesn't split too many verbs, who knows, I may stay awake during the sermon today. I may even give him a few (weak) amens, and a (feeble) hand shake.

God forbid that I or anyone else should question the motives of those who come to church to worship God. Yet, the way some people conduct themselves gives ample cause to wonder. As you and I worship together today, perhaps we can agree that some serious attention needs to be given to these professing but luke-warm Christians. This too is something we must wrestle and fight in the good fight of faith.

The Sense of Self-Sufficiency

We need to fight against the arrogant attitude of the academic over-achiever (know-it-all), the rich, and the powerful, who house the spirit of self-sufficiency. This attitude leads them down the sinful road of unfaithfulness. Having traveled down this road, they may come to believe that there is no God and even if there was a God, that they can and have made it without God. They may loose all desire to be associated with God until tragedy comes knocking at their door. I think you will agree with me that this has, is, and always appears to be a very tough fight. But, thanks be to God, the battle is being fought and won.

The Attitude of Out-of-Sight, Out-of-Mind

We must fight the "out-of-sight, out-of-mind" method of operation. We must not forget the poor, the hungry, the meek, the disinherited, the elderly, the widows, the orphans, and those who feel deserted, abandoned, unloved, and unwanted.

Untrained Attitudes Found in Our Young People

We must fight with the attitude on the part of our young people, that illegal drugs, alcohol, smoking, and getting pregnant as a teenager, or being a mother out of wedlock, is cool, the in-thing, the way to go, or is all right. Do they realize that God is not pleased? We are charged with the responsibility to train-up a child while they are young. Some children will stray away from the fold, but one must consider these questions, "How far will they go? How long will they stay way?"

The Challenge to Change Attitudes

The challenge in attempting to change attitudes is tied in warnings and promises found in God's word. We are warned in God's word to,

> *Be sober, be vigilant; because your adversary the devil walks about like a roaring lion, seeking whom he may devour.* [1 Pet. 5:8]

But, Jesus said,

> *...I have come that they may have life, and that they may have it more abundantly.* [John 10:10]

Psalms 37:4 reads, *"Delight yourself also in the Lord, And He shall give you the desires of your heart."* It is recorded in Psalms 84:11, *"...No good thing will He withhold from those who walk uprightly."* Thank God for being alive and for giving us the opportunity and challenge to fight these destructive attitudes.

Clear Understanding of Faith

Our faith in God should be so clear and strong as to leave no doubt or cause for confusion, or misunderstanding as to who we are in Jesus Christ our Lord and Savior and why we have hope. Sure we may have said we accepted Jesus as Lord and Savior of our lives, but, is that all there is to being a Christian? Is there any commitment? What about the hymn, "Am I a Soldier of the Cross, a follower of the Lamb?" What is that all about?

Am I a soldier of the cross?
A foll'wer of the Lamb?
And shall I fear to own His cause
Or blush to speak His name?

Must I be carried to the skies
On flow'ry beds of ease,
While others fought to win the prize
And sailed thru bloody seas?
Am I a Soldier of the Cross (Issac Watts)

Are these just meaningless words? Our faith in Jesus also makes us warriors in a spiritual battle and the devil is our adversary.

Not only does our faith in God open our eyes to spiritual warfare, it also enables us to walk in the Light of God's truth, to identify the works of the devil, and to be victorious over every challenge that we must face. The battle has already been fought and the victory won in Jesus the Christ. It is only at this point can we even begin to talk about crowns. Our faith opens our eyes to our fight against the wiles of the devil. Our fight against the wiles of the devil will one day be rewarded with crowns. I shall wear a crown, you shall wear a crown. When it's all over, we shall wear a crown. That's right, I got a crown, you got a crown, all God's children got a crown and when we get to heaven we are going to put on our crowns and walk all over God's heaven. In the meantime, we must watch, fight, and pray. To put it simply in a phrase, we have all heard at one time or another, "No cross, No Crown."

BENEDICTION

The

Lord

bless you

and keep you;

The Lord make His face

shine upon you, And be gracious to you;

The Lord lift up His countenance upon you, And give you

peace.

[Numbers 6:24-26]

CRYSTAL FOUNTAIN PUBLICATIONS
P.O. BOX 4434
DIAMOND BAR, CALIFORNIA 91765

ORDER INFORMATION

WHAT IS THIS THING CALLED PREACHING?
An Authentic Collection of Sermons
by Rev. Leon Johnson
Volume One

Leon Johnson
Leonidas A. Johnson

ISBN: 1-889561-01-0 LCCN: 96-85843

Fax orders: (909) 860-7803

Price: $16.95

<u>Discounts</u>:

1	book	no discount
2-4	books	20% discount
5-9	books	30% discount
10-199	books	40% discount
200-499	books	50% discount
500 or more	books	55% discount

Sales Tax: *Please add 8.25% for books shipped to California addresses.*

Shipping: *$4.24 for the first book and $2.17 for each additional book.*

Note: All prices subject to change without notice. Payable in U.S. funds.